PERSONAL POWER

Mindfulness Techniques for the Corporate World

PERSONAL POWER

Mindfulness Techniques for the Corporate World

ROXANA VALEA

Published by RV Publications

A CIP catalogue record for this book is available from the British Library.

ISBN 978-0-9931309-2-2

Contents

Foreword

You have power. You were born with it. You might not believe it because you were not taught to see it. Over the years you may have become accustomed to doing what others expect of you, to thinking that you have very little choice. You might have settled into a life that was less than amazing.

At times, you might have felt this power as a bubbling sensation deep within you, waiting to come to the surface. You might have wondered what it could do, where it could take you, if you just let it out. At other times you might have thought it had gone into hiding, or that it was maybe just sleeping under the surface of a normal life.

And yet it has always been there. Whether you feel it or not, it is still there, deep within you, waiting to be used.

Because no matter what you have done or not done in your life, what you have accomplished or where you have failed, you can always revert back to the power you carry deep within you. Your energy, the power and wisdom you were born with which can take you anywhere you want to go.

This book is a guide to your own power. In seven simple steps you will rediscover where it is, how it works and how you can use it. The first four steps are about increasing your energy, because the quality of what we achieve in our lives is directly proportional to the state of our energy. High vibration energy will push us forward to create the life that we want. Low energy will barely sustain us and only attract similar low vibrations. These steps are all about raising your awareness and the vibration of your energy. You will learn how to ground, how to cleanse and how to protect your energy, and how to trust your intuition. Then, once your energy is strong and stable, you can direct it to create the life that you want.

Steps five to seven deal with manifestation: making things happen. You will learn how to use the power of intent, how to direct your energy to create the life that you want, how to assess the results you are getting and correct your course.

At the end of each chapter you will find suggested exercises to deepen your practice. You can do them as you read through the chapter, or at the end. Or you may decide to read the book first then come back and do the exercises; it's up to you. But one way or the other, make time to do some of them, otherwise the concepts presented in this book won't become anchored.

I have spent more than twenty years in and out of corporate environments as an employee, and later on as a business consultant. I have advised small start-ups as well as giants like Apple, Sony and eBay. I have worked across many industries and geographical locations. I know the pressure those who work in a corporate environment face, the toll it takes on their energy. I have seen what it does to people and I have felt it myself. Over the years it has become clearer and clearer to me that there is a real need for people to get in touch with their own power; to heal themselves, to lead happy and fulfilled lives, while still working in these environments.

This book is a mix of my experiences in the corporate world and my experimentation with the power of intuition and energy. I have personally tried and tested all these steps. Not only have they worked for me, they have also changed my life. I have moved from being a stressed-out consultant permanently on the edge of burnout to a happy and fulfilled individual who mixes work with passion for life in a sustainable way.

At first I started experimenting with a few mindfulness and meditation techniques that allowed me to get in touch with my body and keep my mind still. I slowly added more practices, inspired by yoga, meditation, various lectures I had attended and the courses I have taken to develop my intuition. By trial and error I found out what worked for me and what did not.

I got results. My life improved. I felt more sure of myself, less volatile and less prone to stress. Slowly I solidified these techniques and concepts into seven steps that I started practising daily. The quality of projects I attracted and the calibre of the people that I worked with got better and better. Gradually, I started talking about these steps to other stressed-out corporate people. They told me they got results too. Over the last five years, my tentative attempts have become full routines. I now perform these steps automatically. I know they work for me and for others. I know they can work for you too.

You might already be a big fan of working intuitively, be looking to expand your knowledge and get some additional insights. Or you may be one of the sceptics who think this is just a buzz phrase. Or you might simply feel so tired, so depleted and so lost that you are willing to try anything new. Wherever you are and however you came to this book, I trust that it will help you find your own answers and guide you back to your own power.

PART I
Get Strong

1.

Ground: Find your roots and send them deep

We walk barefoot on a beach. We go to a park in our lunch break, take our shoes off and put our feet on the grass. We let our feet dangle in the water. We feel the sand, the grass or the water between our toes. We instantly feel relieved, as if our worries and anxieties have suddenly gone. In fact, they have. We have discharged them into the ground.

Our body carries electromagnetic energy. As with all energy fields, something happens when we plug it into the ground. We earth it. We discharge it. We let it go. And we are left feeling lighter, healthier and stronger by doing so.

For millions of years people have done this naturally, walking barefoot or simply touching the earth. In today's corporate environments it may be weeks or months before we have the opportunity to feel the grass between our toes. So how do we connect with the earth? And, more importantly, why do we need to do it?

Presence. Where are you?

Before we talk about grounding, about connecting our energy to the earth, we first need to establish where our energy actually is. The easy answer would be that all our energy is with ourselves: it's in our minds, in our body, in our feelings and emotions. But if this is true, why is it that some people seem stronger and more 'together' and others more scattered around? Why is it that we sometimes feel more confident and other times more vulnerable and easily impacted?

Why is it that sometimes we have *presence* and sometimes not?

The dictionary defines presence as 'existing in a place'. The key word here is *a place*. We have presence because we exist *in a place*.

You definitely exist; otherwise you would not be reading this book. But in what *place* are you?

If you close your eyes and ask yourself this question, where does your focus go to immediately?

You may feel your focus is in your head. Or you may even feel that your focus points to a place outside your head, somewhere high up in the air. Does your focus go to your body when you ask this question? If so, where exactly does it point? Is it your chest, your belly, your legs? Are you outside or inside your body?

Our bio-magnetic energy extends around our body roughly the distance of our arms when stretched apart. This is our personal space. It's part of us. We share this only with people we feel intimate with and feel invaded when others don't respect it. This space holds our energy as well. It may be that the bulk of our focus is outside our physical body, located somewhere within our personal space. As I wrote this paragraph, I paused and asked myself this question. I immediately felt the core of my energy was somewhere outside my body to the right roughly at the same level with my throat. This is where I am right now.

It all starts with awareness. Know where your focus is, where your energy is concentrated. Notice how this changes during the day. Where you are in the office might not be the same place you are when at home. Get used to asking yourself this question day after day, hour after hour.

Where am I right now?

With no judgement, no pressure and no feeling of right or wrong, ask yourself this question and notice where you are.

I feel the sweat building on my forehead. Once I stand up, in the light of the projector, everybody will be able to see it and then everybody will know how scared I actually feel.

"Stop it!" I tell myself. "Think about the slides, the words. Think about what you need to say." I rehearsed this presentation a thousand times, I knew well what I wanted to say. What I don't know is how they will take it, what they will say and what they will ask me. So I'm spending my last minutes before my presentation desperately trying to guess their reaction.

We are a team of consultants giving a presentation to the board of a major organisation that has hired us for restructuring advice. Each of us presents one area: our work, our findings and our recommendations. Each of us has about ten slides to go through. I have rehearsed mine hundreds of times before.

My colleague is almost done with his part. I have not heard one word he has said. I have been practising over and over again what I am about to say when my turn comes. And I have worried again and again about how I might look and sound to them, and more importantly about one key question: will they like me? Will they think I am good enough?

I should know what I am supposed to say, I tell myself, and I know this is true. I do know what I am about to present. The content of my slides is not the issue; this is not what makes me sweat now and fills me with anxiety.

The issue is that I am not actually here.

I am not here as I wait for my turn and I am not here as I stand up, walk towards the front of the room and take my place beside the projector. I am not actually here as I press 'enter' to show the first of my slides, or as I take in a small breath and begin to talk in a voice that sounds, to me, filled with dread and uncertainty. One thought comes back again and again, no matter how hard I push it away: will they notice how nervous I am?

I am not here, because a part of me has left my body. It has travelled the length of the room and has gone into the heads of the people watching me. One part of me is now inside the head of each of the twenty faces watching me as I painfully struggle to explain the first slide of my presentation. I am in their heads, I am behind their eyes, I am there trying to see myself as they see me, trying to imagine what they think about me. I am not me. I am trying to be them. I am the judgements I imagine and the approvals I seek.

The next fifteen minutes go by in a blur. I read the slides, point out the facts. I say what I need to say, what I practised so many times before. I painfully go through my presentation one slide at a time. And as I reach the end of it, I think I should feel relieved: I have done it. Actually someone else has done it, not me. I was not there; I was lost in the head of all these important people, the board of directors of the organisation that hired us. Only the leftovers of me were on that stage, mechanically pressing 'enter' to show a new slide and talking in a low, monotonous voice.

I sit down at the end of the presentation and the feeling of dread is not gone. It is still there, sitting down with me, telling me I could have done better.

I wish someone had told me about presence in the early days of my consulting career. That someone had warned me to be aware of where I am. I would have realised that I was not in my body when giving a presentation; I would have understood what it does to me when I leave my body and scatter my energy around.

You probably know what it does to you too. You know when you have given a good presentation and when you have not. When you have made a difference in a meeting and when you have not. When you could stand your ground easily and when you have been run over. Deep within you, whether you admit it or not, you know when it felt good, powerful and easy and when it did not. You may not know why, but the feeling of 'this went well and it was easy' is very clearly different from the feeling of 'I wonder what they thought about this?'

One is a feeling of power, the other is a feeling of struggle.

When you identify the feeling of struggle, ask yourself immediately: where am I? Where is my focus? And once you have found the exact place where your energy is located at that moment, it is time to go further: call your energy home.

Turn to the end of the chapter and do exercise 1.1.

Calling your energy home

Practising the awareness exercise might show you that your focus is inside your body most of the time and that you feel well and at home there. If so, that's great, you can skip this part and go straight to growing your roots. But if you found out that you are not in your body or that your focus wanders outside, it's time to call it home.

Call your energy home by focusing on the parts of yourself that you have identified as being outside your body. Set the intention to have them return to you. Instruct them to come back to your body. Imagine every little particle of your energy that you have given or sent away coming back home to you.

Pieces of you may be scattered everywhere. They may be with the worry you have left with someone else, the piece of you trying to see yourself through the eyes of your audience as you give a presentation, the part of you that was left quarrelling with the driver that scratched your car as you drove to work that morning. Just bring back the focus inside yourself. Feel your thoughts and your emotions coming back to you. One little shortcut to help you do this: become aware of your breathing as you hold the intention in your mind to call your energy home.

Had I have known how to do this as I stumbled through my slides in front of that board of directors, I would have realised I was not inside my body in the first place. I would have remembered to ask myself the question, where am I right now? I would have then realised a little piece of me was in the head of all those powerful executives. I would have closed my eyes briefly for just a second and said in my mind: "I call all my energy home, all the pieces of myself that I have sent away, I call them back inside my own body." I would have seen them return to me in any form that I could have imagined, be it as rays of light, balls of fire or as an elastic band snapping back. I would have tried to imagine how they would feel when they came back. Warm? Cool? Fresh? I would have imagined those particles of me actually coming back to me and felt them getting inside my body. And I would have asked myself again the same question, just to double check: "Where am I right now?" And I would have kept on doing it as I paused to press enter for a new slide or as I took a breath before I answered a question from the audience. I would have done it again and again until the consistent response that I would have got for my question would have been "I am inside my body".

Calling your energy home is done with intention. Simply say it in your mind. "I am calling my energy home. From wherever I have scattered it. From the people who are listening to my speech right now, from my boss, from my group of friends, from my spouse, from my family, from my sick dog at home. I am calling my energy home." Then feel it, or visualise it coming back to you and being absorbed by your body. If it's a piece of you it has no place in someone else's head. If it's a piece of you it should be with you, so that you are whole.

When you feel scattered around, just bring your attention back to yourself, to your body. Energy follows thought so it will do whatever you instruct it to do.

As you do this, know that this will by no means make you a less caring or empathetic person. You can still listen to someone and empathise with them while holding your energy inside yourself. You can still love someone and want the best for them but do so with all your energy home. You can be whole energetically and be fully opened up to nature or to playing with your child, or to connecting with people and animals.

Calling your energy home does not mean cutting yourself off from everything around you and focusing obsessively on your own self. On the contrary: by having your entire energy home, you are becoming more available to authentically open up and connect to others. The only difference is that you will do so from a place of personal power.

Turn to the end of the chapter and do exercise 1.2.

Get into your body

If you're used to scattering pieces of yourself habitually as you go through your day, you may feel overwhelmed by all this energy returning to you.

Before, you used to have a coffee and read the paper. Part of you was going away with the stories you read. Before, you may not have called them back once you finished the story. Now you do. Before, you might have left a piece of yourself hanging by the coffee machine in the office, right there where you met that colleague you wanted to impress. Now you call it home. The question is, what do you do with all these parts of yourself that are now crowding around you? They may feel uncomfortable as they come back. You may not be used to them and for a second you may even think about sending them away again. Before you are tempted to do so, just try this: send them down instead.

Grounding is the process of gathering your energy from wherever you might have left it scattered, getting it back inside your body and once there, sending it deep down towards the centre of the earth. Just like a plant, you grow your roots and send them deep into the ground.

This applies to all the parts of yourself coming home, as well as to the bulk of your energy if you are one of those who is hovering around your own head most of the time. Bring your awareness inside your body, first into your head, and then let it go down into your body. See it travel through your neck, down into your shoulders and arms, and even lower, into your chest around your heart. Find the centre of your body, the point that is three fingers down from your navel and three fingers back from the skin. This place is referred to as the Hara by the martial arts masters and it's thought to be the centre of balance in our body. Try locating your energy there and feel the difference it makes to your self-confidence. Remember this point – it is the centre of your body power.

For a long time, many of us in the corporate world have been used to operating as talking heads only. It might feel very uncomfortable to get in touch with your body at first, to realise that the bulk of you exists from your neck down. If you have spent years outside your body, you may regard it as a stranger. But it pays to get used to it. Holding your energy inside your body rather than outside requires patience more than anything else. The old habits will try to come back for a while. When they do, just remember to check where your energy is, call it home and get it back inside your body. Then get acquainted with it, make peace with it.

When you are mostly outside your body or ungrounded, you may experience some of the following symptoms:

- Dizzy, hypoglycaemic, low blood pressure
- Unpunctual, chaotic, disorganised, forgetful
- Hyperactive and always in a rush, or tired all the time
- Lack of body awareness, clumsy, easily bruised
- Getting lots of electric shocks
- Not doing what you say you will
- Not listening, cannot take in information, cannot concentrate
- Anxiety, panic, fear or emotional numbness
- Unable to relax or sit still
- Insomnia
- Jumping very easily when there is noise or sudden movement
- Oversensitive to light

- Getting frequent colds and other illnesses
- Being irritable, angry and aggressive
- Absorbing energy from other people and places
- Finding it hard to meditate and still the mind

As you get your energy inside your body, a few things are likely to happen:

- First, you will have more weight. I don't mean you will put on weight: quite the contrary actually. Ungrounded people tend to put on weight easily, to compensate for their lack of grounding. No, what I mean is that you will have more weight in the eyes of others. Something miraculous will have happened. Others will start perceiving the energy you pushed down through your body. They will perceive your weight. The weight behind your words, your ideas, your deeds and your decisions. You will become more visible, more important. People will start thinking they should not mess with you because you have *weight*.

- Second, you will feel more anchored, more sure about what you want, what you say and what you choose to do. It's the difference between operating from the inside rather than the outside. Your power resides inside you. Once you start sending your energy inside your body, you start tapping into your personal power.

- Third, you will find doing things becomes easier. While before you needed to deploy a lot more energy to get things done, you will find that your body easily provides that source of energy now. Why? Because by being inside your body, you automatically tap into the energy that the body generates. It was always there, only you might not have fully connected to it before. But now you have and you'll notice the difference.

Turn to the end of the chapter and do exercise 1.3.

Grow your roots

As soon as you get inside your body, people will start to see a change in you. You might get noticed more often at work, people might remember your name, your face, a comment you made in a meeting. They might congratulate you on a presentation you've given. They will make themselves available to talk to you. Your presence and your magnetism will have increased simply because you are inside your body now, connected to all its power. This, in itself, is magnetic to other people.

Your voice might change too. If you consistently send your energy down inside your body when you speak to an audience

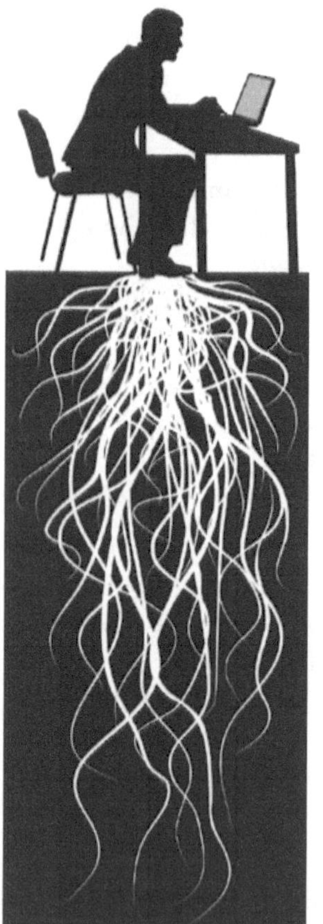

or deliver your presentation, your voice will carry more weight. You will not need to struggle to gain attention. The lower in your body you visualise your voice originating from, the more weight it will have. It will be supported by all the weight of your body. Next time when you deliver a presentation, keep focusing on the soles of your feet as you speak and see what that does to your level of self-confidence and to your voice.

When you are inside your body and well connected to it, you are likely to feel safe. Protected. You may no longer dread your weekly meeting with a bullying boss. Inside your body, you are in your power base. Your energy is home. The whole of you is home. You feel good. No one is going to come for you in there.

The next step once you are inside your body is to grow your roots and anchor yourself firmly in the earth.

Imagine you are a plant and grow your roots from each of the soles of your feet, as well as from the base of your spine, going into the floor. Just close your eyes and visualise them in whatever shape or colour they come to you. Allow yourself to have fun with it. This is your private movie; no one needs to know what happens in your head!

Imagine your roots travelling through your clothes and your shoes, right though the chair you are sitting on. See them piercing the carpet and the floor, going down through the floors until they reach the foundation of the building. Once there, they cut through the concrete and the steel, the bricks and the sand until they reach the earth that's underneath it all. And when they reach the earth they keep on going, growing deep into the ground like the strong roots of a tree or however you want to see them in your mind. They go down deeper and deeper still, through the various layers of the earth, through rock and through sand, through layers beneath layers, deeper and deeper. Use the power of your imagination to see them going down.

They keep going until they reach the centre of the earth.

How do you know you have reached the centre of the earth? You just ask. Is this all there is? Can I go any deeper? If you feel like you can go deeper, continue. Grow your roots, send them down with the power of your imagination and remember: energy follows thought. You are where you direct your focus to be. Send your imagination deep down into the earth and your energy will actually *be* there.

When you feel like you have reached the centre of the earth, try to visualise it. See how it comes to you. It's easiest to imagine it as a rock, a big, solid rock. But again, play with your imagination, set it free. If you prefer to see it as an orange, go for it. It's your orange. And who am I to say the centre of the earth should be one big, solid rock? I have only been there inside my own head.

It is very important that you develop your own way to visualise your grounding. You can start with imagining roots going deep and seeing the centre of the earth as one big, solid rock. But as you get more comfortable with it you can change roots for ropes or cables or anchors, and you can see the centre of the earth in different shapes and colours. Don't be afraid to experiment. Whatever works for you is fine. Just use images and symbols that give you a sense you are safely anchored to the centre of the earth.

When you arrive at the centre of the earth, connect with it. Plant your roots there, throw your anchors in, tie your ropes, put a padlock on your chain. Whatever you need to do, do it. Just make sure you connect yourself to the centre of the earth and that the connection is secure.

In your mind, hold the thought that you are connected and anchored there. Know this is where you originate from, that you can come back through those roots at any time you choose, and that all the power of the earth is travelling up your roots, into your body, and it is there for you to use.

Then come back up, into your body, into the presentation room where you are speaking, back to your audience, and see what that has done to you, how you feel, and how the people around you respond to you now.

If you have already felt the difference in how you move, talk and work when you are in your body compared to when your energy was scattered outside your body, you will most likely feel this additional energy boost. The power of the earth is so much more than we can habitually hold in our bodies. And the beauty of it is that it's available for all of us to tap into.

Is it that easy? You may wonder. It is. Remember, energy follows thought. When you imagine you are connected to the centre of the earth, you actually are. Once you visualise your roots, your ropes or your anchors, you actually have them. All it takes is some practise and the faith that it works.

It may sound silly but it actually works. That's because the brain cannot perceive the difference between real and imagined events. If you want to convince yourself, just bring to mind the image of a freshly cut lemon, imagine squeezing its juice on to your tongue and see what immediate response you get in your mouth.

Try grounding before a big presentation, before you walk into an important meeting or before a difficult phone call. Try it out when you feel unable to say no. Try it when someone is attempting to bully you or before you ask for a pay rise. Or before you stand up to deliver a speech. Try it when you need to make a decision that you have been postponing for some time. Just try it and see what happens.

He was not shouting any longer but the silence now seemed even more threatening than the emotional unleash just minutes before. Will he hit me? I thought. Will he actually dare to hit me, right here and now as we both stand looking into each other's eyes, both of us wearing business suits in the middle of this meeting room, with the flipchart still bearing his handwriting abandoned in the corner?

His face was close, very close, his nose almost touching mine. I could feel the heat of his skin. I could see the sweat on his forehead, clearly, like drops of rain on a leaf. I could sense the deep, burning anger in his eyes.

And if he hits me, what will I do? My mind continued to race, desperate to fill the heavy silence around us. Will I hit him back? Will we actually, physically have a fight? Two consultants on the same team who are here to deliver a project for this client? Will we pull each other's hair out and hit each other in the middle of the clients' meeting room, with busy people walking down the corridor just outside the door? Will he hit me in here knowing that someone can come in any time if I scream? Does he really care?

I think this is what he had in mind when he asked everyone to leave the room. He was the project manager, of course they obeyed. He was my manager, I had challenged him in the middle of the team meeting and he did not like it. I had told him that his approach would not work for my area and I had explained – to him as well to the others

– efficiently and calmly why I thought so. He did not take that well. I could hear his breath starting to quicken as I talked and I could sense the anger in him building up as he left the flipchart he was writing on and started walking towards me.

I had publicly defied him and I knew I was on dangerous ground. A few days before I had privately defied him in an email and I was aware he had still not digested this. Then, as well as now, I had explained exactly why I could not do what he wanted me to do. But this time he was not prepared to take it. And I expected his anger. But I did not expect what came next. He lost his temper and started shouting, he called me names, he threatened, he tried to intimidate me. I told him there was no need to get angry just because he did not agree with me and it was that which had pushed him over the edge. He turned around and asked everyone to leave the room. They did. All but one. One older lady, an outside contractor, a psychologist hired to deliver a specific piece of our assessment for that client. She did not move: she simply took out a piece of paper and started writing, deeply absorbed in the details of it as if the two of us were not there in the same room with her. I did not know if I felt relieved or embarrassed by her presence. Will he hit me in front of her? I wondered.

"I think you should sit down and have a glass of water," I told him. "It's dangerous getting angry like that. You might have a heart attack or something."

He did not hit me but he screamed as if he was out of his mind. I watched him and I let him do it. By then I knew he would not hit me. For some inexplicable reason I felt suddenly safe, as if I was no longer in that room... I was going down, deep down towards the centre of the earth, travelling with my roots. I did not know what I was doing but it felt safer to go there. I let him scream all that he had to scream and simply watched him do it and wondered what was it that stopped him from hitting me as he so obviously wished to do. From deep down there, from the secure place I had found in the centre of the earth, I watched him drown in his own fury and I watched the old lady as she wrote down everything that she was witnessing.

I was still there, deeply anchored into my roots, when he decided to leave and slammed the door, and I was still there, on that project, weeks after he was fired that very same evening following the report the old woman had filed against him.

I did not know it then but it was his threat that helped me find my roots.

Grounding may take some practise to perfect but once you know how to get there you will go back easily whenever you need it. There are many times during the day when you can go there just to visit your power base. Take a tour to the centre of the earth and come back feeling strong.

This is not a secret. Sportspeople know all about grounding. They know if and when they are grounded and when not. A martial arts fighter will not go far without grounding. A polo player will come off the saddle, a rugby player will be blown off his feet and a surfer will lose his balance on the wave. All these sports have one thing in common. They teach you to ground.

This is not something only available to you or me. Just like taking your shoes off and walking barefoot on the grass, it is available to all of us. It conjures a similar feeling in all of us. The difference is that while many of us think about it, only few do it, and fewer still do it often enough.

When you start doing this you might find out that you have done it before and you did not know what it was you were doing. You might feel like you are revisiting a very familiar place. You can do it consciously now. Or you may feel like you have always felt such a place of safety existed but you have never actually been there before. Explore and enjoy! It is yours to use any time you want. Whether new or not, know that you have the option to return to this place any time you choose. And the more often you go there, the easier it is to access it when you need it.

If you take one thing from this book, let it be grounding. It is the first step in becoming conscious of your power and starting to use it. It can also be used by itself. Grounding is where it all starts. Find your connection to the earth and use it often. It will change your life.

Turn to the end of the chapter and do exercise 1.4.

How to use grounding

The real beauty about going deep and finding the energy of the earth is that you can actually use it. It is there, available to all. You can pull it up through your roots when you feel tired or depleted just as a plant would pull up water. You can use it when you need a boost.

It can help you to push through the last hours of work when you would rather be somewhere else, doing something else. Or it will give you enough energy to write the last few pages of the long report you've been working on. Or simply make it to the end of a very boring presentation. When you need that extra little bit of help, remember that it's readily available for you just under your chair. Get into your body, send your roots down, find the centre of the earth and connect with it. And once you're there, pull up its energy and let it travel up and down your body, let it energise and refresh you.

Once you have found your own method of grounding and have practised it a few times, you'll realise it gets easier and easier. It's like training a muscle or your mind to do something new. Only now you're training your energy to come home and become solidly anchored to the centre of the earth.

Turn to the end of the chapter and do exercise 1.5.

What you can ground

You can use grounding not only for yourself but for other objects around you as well.

Spaces

Just as you ground your own energy, you can ground the energy of a room, desk, office or building using their roots. Imagine the space you want to ground has its own roots and they travel down just like your roots do. Close your eyes, do your own grounding visualisation, then imagine the roots of the space you want to ground travelling to the centre of the earth. Tie them securely there. Just keep in mind that your roots and the roots of the space you want to ground are two different things. Keep them separate.

What I find particularly useful in business is to ground a meeting room before a meeting takes place there. Even if the other participants are not aware of this, when they walk into a meeting room that has been grounded they will feel that space vibrates differently. Negative energy, anxiety or negative emotions will be released into the ground. Participants will feel more in touch with their own selves and with the purpose of that meeting. This happens because the room's energy is now connected to the earth. They will feel lighter, more focused and more productive. Grounding a meeting room cannot replace an individual's own grounding practices but it can help with the overall efficiency and focus of a meeting and make it easier to achieve its purpose.

You can also ground conference calls as a virtual space where participants meet. Just imagine it as a virtual meeting room, visualise its roots and take them down towards the centre of the earth at the same time as you send your own roots down. The difference you will find in terms of the quality of interaction will be noticeable.

One word of warning: ground only what's yours. We will talk more about using energy responsibly in Chapter 7 but for now, a principle you need to keep in mind for all you are doing is that you are responsible for your own energy, and that of your children, but no one else's. Do not ground someone else's desk, house, or room without their explicit permission. You can ground a meeting room if you have called the meeting and you are chairing it or if you are responsible for it but not if it is someone else's meeting and they are not aware of what you are doing. Ground yourself and not another person, unless they ask you to do so. Interfering with another person's energy is energy manipulation and it can have negative effects both on you and the other person.

Projects, plans, ideas

Just like spaces, projects, plans and ideas can be grounded. It will increase their energy; they will gain more weight. Just like a plant plugged into the soil, they will grow more easily and with far less effort.

You can do it in just the same way as with spaces. Imagine the project, the plan or the idea in whatever shape you want. It can be as a written report, a presentation or an Excel spreadsheet with the key figures of a business plan. Visualise it. Then imagine its roots growing from the base of that object. Take the roots down towards the centre of the earth. Tie them securely to the rock you find in the centre of the earth. See the visual shape of the project, plan or idea securely bound to the centre of the earth. In your mind, see its roots strong and healthy. See them reaching out deep into the ground and tied securely to the centre of the earth.

You can ground business plans for new ventures, project plans, new product ideas, a book or a blog you are writing. Ground them at various stages in their lifetimes and check their grounding often. Remember, their roots are their own, not yours. You are not your plans, projects and ideas: allow them to have separate roots and tie those securely into the centre of the earth. Allow them to grow, to flourish, but also allow them to disappear and die if that is what's best for you and for them. We will talk more about manifestation later in the book. For now, just know that you can ground them and that this can help them grow.

Again, remember to ground only what is yours unless the owner of the plan, project or idea has specifically asked for your help and knows what you are doing. Don't walk around trying to ground the world around you. You will become depleted before you know it.

When you need a little help

Grounding is a mental game but in addition to the visualisation techniques described, there are other things you can use when you need some help:

Food

Some foods unground you naturally. Alcohol is the most notable of these. Ground before and after you drink alcohol and be aware of the effect it has on your energy. Some other foods will help you ground: all root vegetables – potatoes, onions, carrots, etc. carry the energetic imprint to take you back into the earth. Salts and minerals found in the earth will take your energy back there and so will green vegetables growing close to the ground. Other grounding foods include any root-based teas, almonds and nuts, as well as carbohydrates and organic protein sources. Vitamin C is an important grounding aid and any foods that contain it will help you ground. But the most important nutrient you can get into your body to help you ground it is pure water, and plenty of it.

Sports

Any type of physical activity is an excellent way to get in touch with your body and actually feel it. The muscle pain you get as you exercise might be just what you need to release old emotions you have stored. The body awareness that sports require is an excellent help to direct your attention to your body, become accustomed to it and learn to listen to it. As you get to know your body through sports, remember that where you focus is where you actually are: energy follows thought. Even light exercise like walking or cycling will have an important effect on your grounding, as will being in nature or gardening.

Meditation

Find one meditation technique that works for you and make it a regular practice. It can be as little as five minutes per day. Focus on practices that emphasise the use of the senses – look, listen, taste, smell, touch. There are many alternatives out there and what works for one person will not work for another. Try a few and find your way.

Others

Wearing certain colours will help your grounding, specifically red, brown, black and green. Homeopathy enthusiasts will find arnica and oak remedies help with grounding, as well as the Bach flower essence clematis. Certain crystals like haematite and brown, black or dark green stones help grounding too.

Summary: How to ground

- Become aware of your energy and where it is concentrated.
- Notice when pieces of you are scattered around and call them home.
- Get inside your body, feel it and send your energy inside and down through your body.
- Visualise growing roots and sending them deep into the centre of the earth.
- Tie your roots securely to the centre of the earth and feel solidly anchored.
- Use the energy of the earth by pulling it up through your roots just like a plant pulls up water from the ground.
- Use the same grounding technique to ground objects or concepts that are yours or that you are personally responsible for.

Grounding Exercises:

> **1.1 Practise becoming aware of your energy and where it is concentrated:**

- Throughout the day, ask yourself frequently: where am I right now?

- Notice the first place that comes to you.

- Notice if you are outside or inside your body.

- If you are outside your body, where is it that you have left your energy? Are you at home replaying the morning argument you had with your partner? Are you at your child's school, worrying that you will be late to work? Have you left a piece of you stuck to the TV, watching this morning's news?

- If you are inside your body, which part of your body is it that holds the core of your energy in this moment? The head? The chest? The belly?

- As you notice where you are, also notice how you feel when you are there.

- Let go of any judgements regarding right or wrong; just become aware of where you are and how it feels to be there.

> **1.2 Became aware when pieces of you are scattered around and practise calling them home:**

- Visualise the pieces of your energy that you have identified are not with you.

- Close your eyes and say in your mind: I am calling my energy home.

- Focus on your breath as you say this. Feel yourself inhale and exhale.

- Visualise these parts of you coming back to you. Use any image that comes to you. Be creative and have fun with it.

- Feel them coming back and actually entering your body. Be curious. Ask yourself, how do they feel?

- Keep focusing on your breath as you call your energy home.

- Ask again: where am I? Do this until you get the answer: Here, inside your body.

1.3 Practise sending your energy down into your body:

- If you feel your focus is inside the head, try to feel your heart. Anything below the neck would do, for a start.

- Give yourself time to get used to the new feeling, then go lower.

- From the heart go to your stomach, then lower, inside the abdomen. Try to find the Hara point located just below the navel and about three fingers inside your body. See how you feel when you centre your focus there.

- Deepen your body awareness by using your senses. Take a moment to sit down. Focus your eyes softly on something: it can be anything. Listen to the sounds you hear. Feel the sensation of touch: it can be as simple as just rubbing two fingers together. Keep on looking, listening and feeling. If your mind wanders, bring it back. Don't fight it, just bring it back. Keep on looking, listening and feeling. You are back in your body while you do this.

- Notice and learn how it feels to be in various parts of your body; where you feel more relaxed and where less; what makes you stronger and what doesn't.

1.4 Practise feeling your roots and sending them down into the centre of the earth:

- Find a quiet place to spend five minutes every morning after you wake up, or every evening before you go to bed.

- Sit down on a chair with the soles of your feet fully touching the ground, preferably barefoot. Or sit cross-legged on the floor on a pillow. Use whatever sitting position is easiest for you and allows you to have contact with the floor. Try to be as close as possible to the floor.

- Close your eyes. Focus on your breath; feel your breath as you inhale and as you exhale.

- Become aware where your focus is and call your energy home. Do this by saying in your mind "I am calling my energy home" and then visualise it arriving back to you.

- Bring your attention to your body and find your core, ideally the Hara point that lies just below our navel and about three fingers inside your abdomen. Feel how it feels to be there.

- Take a deep breath.

- As you exhale, feel your roots growing from the base of your spine and from each foot. Visualise or sense them in any way that is meaningful or easy for you. They can be roots, anchors, cords, chains. The more solid the material, the better.

- Send them down; see them travelling downwards through the ground towards the centre of the earth. Visualise their journey as if it's a movie or a cartoon. If you are more inclined to sensing rather than visualising, notice how it feels to travel through layers of earth and stone as they go deeper and deeper.

- Take a few deep breaths. Every time you exhale, let your roots go deeper.

- Keep on visualising or sensing their journey. Go deeper and deeper until you feel you have arrived at the centre of the earth.

- See how this looks to you. When you try this for the first few times, it is helpful if you imagine it as a big rock. Make this rock the colour that you want. Feel its heaviness and its power.

- Bind your roots to this rock. Make as many knots as you want. Secure them safely.
- Then come back up, inside your body, and know that you are grounded and connected to the centre of the earth. And that you are safe.
- Carry on with your day, remembering that you are securely anchored to the centre of the earth.

1.5 Practice using the energy of the earth:

- As you connect to the centre of the earth, sense its energy. Sense the huge, amazing power and stability it has. Know this is available for you to use.
- Pull it up through your roots, just like a plant would pull water from the earth.
- Do this as you breathe in. Take a few breaths, feeling this energy of the earth coming into your body travelling up and down your legs, up and down your spine.
- Feel its power inside your body. Enjoy it. It's yours to use. It can clear lower vibrations from the body or melt tension. Use your imagination, follow your intuition, and you will discover many ways in which it can assist you. Trust that what you are imagining is actually happening.
- Throughout the day, pause to take energy from the earth whenever you need an extra boost. Feel this energy flowing into your body, rejuvenating you, giving you power. Know that it is there for you whenever you need it.

Note: most of the exercises in this book will ask you to visualise or imagine things. If you are not a visual person, don't worry, there are other ways to go about them. Try sensing them instead, feeling a sensation. If this feels difficult as well, just have an intention to feel them in any way that is appropriate for you. Hold this thought as you do the exercises. This will be enough.

2

Cleanse: Let go of what you no longer need

We take a shower every morning. It makes us feel lighter, refreshed, reenergised. We wash our clothes. We clean and declutter our homes.

We do this because we feel the need for a fresh, clean start. Well, it's the same with our energy. Just as we care for our body and possessions, cleaning our energy on a regular basis will make us feel lighter, stronger and fresher.

As discussed in Chapter 1, our energy extends all around us. It's our personal space, about the size of our outstretched arms around our body. Some people call it aura. Others can actually see it. Most of us can feel it. When someone enters our personal space we become acutely aware that we either like it or we don't. This happens because it touches our energy field.

Our energy field holds the imprint of our thoughts and emotions, as well as those of others around us – particularly if they are directed at us. If someone thinks badly of us, they will leave an imprint into our energy. If someone sends us loving thoughts, they will leave an imprint as well. If someone tries to manipulate us, they will do it consciously or unconsciously by trying to interfere with our energy. People can connect to our energy just like they would connect to us physically, by touch. Instead of physically pushing, they can also pull the cords they have sent into our energy to make us take a certain action. This is how manipulation works at an energy level.

There are days when we feel overloaded, as if we carry the world on our shoulders. Chances are we have taken an energy load. Other days we feel lighter, as if we have shed some weight. Chances are we have indeed.

This chapter is about learning to do that consciously, about identifying what is in our energy fields, what impacts us, and choosing what we keep and what we let go of.

What impacts our energy?

People

The biggest impact on our energy comes from the people around us. Just like we might have sent parts of us to them when we scattered our energy, so have they sent parts of their energy to us, maybe trying to impress us, to make us like them, to influence us to do certain things. They have thought about us and their thoughts have impacted upon us. They experienced emotions relating to us and a part of those emotions lingered in our energy field. They talked to us or about us and the energy of those words is with us.

People impact upon other people constantly, with or without being aware of what they are doing. The expectations they have of you are real, powerful energies they send to you. Consciously or unconsciously, you pick them up and carry them with you, until you learn to choose what you keep and what you leave.

In the corporate environment, the impact of people's energy is considerably higher than in everyday life. That's because people depend on each other to make things happen, to launch projects, to deliver results, to get paid, to get a promotion, to get that bonus. In the corporate world people form alliances and break them, according to how their interests change; support each other and then turn against each other. Backstabbing and betrayals are common, but so is real support and teamwork. Competitors hope your new product line will not launch. This energy enters your field, particularly if you are directly involved with the new product line. A rival colleague secretly hopes your project will fail and his succeeds so that he gets the promotion and you don't. The energy he sends enters your field. Your boss really needs to report a success back to the board and desperately hopes you manage to close that deal before the end of the quarter. His energy enters your field.

Whatever the reason and whatever the purpose, there is a massive shift of energies among people working in the corporate environment and you are likely to be significantly impacted by all of this, whether you are aware of it or not.

Places

The environment we live and work in has a massive impact on our energy. If the building where we go to work every day used to be a prison in the past, it will still carry the energy of all those imprisoned there. If it does not have enough sunlight and no fresh air, its energy will become stagnant and it will impact the energy of the people working there. If the meeting room you just entered happened to host a very aggressive debate just an hour before, it will still carry that energy and likely it will impact the participants in the next meeting even if they are unaware of it.

Energy discharged into a space will stay there for a while and will impact the energy of whoever passes by that space unless they are aware and protected.

Thoughts

Remember, energy follows thought. Our own thoughts will highly impact our own energy, as well as that of people we direct them to. If we think we will fail, we are programming ourselves to do so. If we worry we'll be late, we are increasing our chance of being late. If we genuinely want someone to succeed, we are sending them an energy load that will actually help them succeed. Minute after minute and hour after hour, our thoughts generate energy no matter how quickly they pass through our head. Becoming aware of what we are generating for us and for others is one of the most empowering tools we can use.

The body

The food we eat, the quality of our sleep and the health of our body will impact our energetic field. A body that moves creates high vibration. A body that sits on a chair the whole day will make the energy stagnant. Food that nurtures us raises our energy. Lack of sleep depletes it. Day after day, each and every decision we make about our body impacts the level of energy we are producing and hence the amount of energy we have available to create the life that we want. People who are habitually not fully living in their bodies tend to be less aware of the impact these choices have on their body. But once you connect with your body and ground it regularly, you are likely to improve the quality of decisions you make about food, sleep or exercise.

How to clean our energy

Before we attempt to clean our energy it is essential that we first become aware of the state it is in. How do we feel, physically and emotionally? How do we feel in certain places, with certain people? How do we feel when we enter a certain meeting room?

Become aware of when you feel good and when you don't, even if you have no explanation as to why. Become aware if all of a sudden you feel low on energy. Before you reach out for that cup of coffee or snack, just become aware of it. Tell yourself "I am feeling my energy going down right now". You may already know why. That's great. If you don't know why, just notice it.

Noticing gives us power. It's the most important step. If we know what is going on we can do something about it. If we don't, we have no chance. Noticing helps even if we don't do something about it immediately. Sometimes all we need is a good night's sleep. Some other times though, we need a little bit more.

There are many methods to cleanse our energy field and each will appeal to certain individuals. Just as with grounding, it is important that you find your own way to do this. The following techniques are suggestions to help you experiment and see what works for you.

The disk of white light

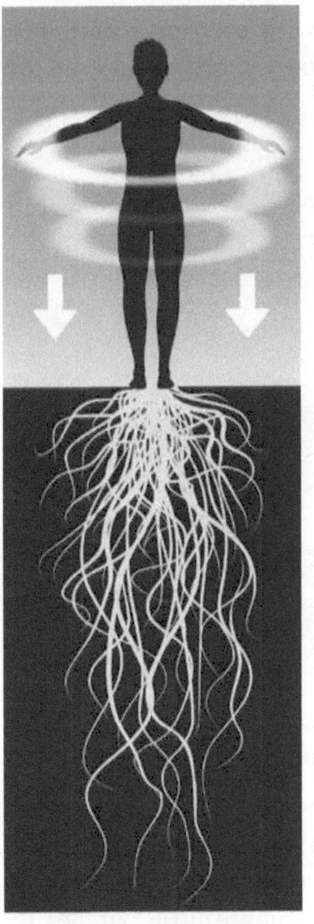

Imagine a disk of white light coming from the centre of the earth, right from the place where you connected your roots, coming up and travelling through and around your body from your feet up to your head and then lifting up into the sky and going as high as it can until it dissolves into white light. This disk cleans all impurities inside and around your body and dissolves them into white light. Then, imagine a disk of white light above your head, about as wide as your body with your arms stretched out. Bring it down this time, pass it through and around your body starting with your head and ending with your feet, and visualise how it gathers all impurities, all negativities, all that needs to leave your body. Then send the disk to the centre of the earth and burn it there. As you do this, hold the intention that its energy gets transmuted into beneficial energy for the earth.

The body scan

Scan your body, starting with the top of your head. Feel the skin on your skull. Bathe it in white light, relax it, see and feel it relaxing. Continue with your hair, your skull, your forehead, your eyes, inside and out, until you visualise your eyelids relaxed and bathed in white light; your ears, your nose, your cheeks. Continue with your neck, your shoulders, your right arm up to the tips of our fingers, your left arm. Go down your body piece by piece and mentally relax, stretch and cleanse each part of your body using white light. Then go inside and do the same with the internal organs. Stay with each part until you feel it relax. Try to feel each part as you visualise it and see the white light that cleanses and bathes it. When you reach your toes, end with a quick shower of white light.

The white light shower

This method is quicker and it works great for when you have not got a lot of time. Imagine yourself under a shower of pure white light. Feel how it cleanses you, how it washes away any negativity that might reside in your energy. See all energy dirt going down a drain. Keep the shower going until you feel light and clean.

Turn to the end of the chapter and do exercise 2.1.

It is important to have fun as you experiment with these methods. There are infinite ways in which you can imagine cleansing your energy. Some people visualise little patches or stains in their energy field and wash them away. Some imagine the negative energies we carry around as little objects that hang off our energy field and imagine picking them off. Some others send a white disk upwards towards the sky and dissolve it in pure white light, while others send it downwards and burn it in the centre of the earth.

Whatever you want to do, just do it. Whatever comes to your mind, trust it. Remember, this is your private encounter with yourself. You don't need to explain this to anyone. If you want to use your favourite image from a cartoon you watched when you were five years old, do it. Keep your intention to cleanse your energy field and imagine this in any way that is meaningful to you.

You might not be a visual person and you might find it more difficult to imagine things. If this is the case, don't despair; just sense it. Feel it, feel your skin and beyond getting cleansed under a shower of white light. Feel the sensation of shedding a weight off your shoulders. You don't need to visualise it. Just feel it. And if you are not very sure you can feel it, just think about it. A thought is a form of energy and it's enough to affect your energy. Above all, don't stress about it. Whether you can visualise, sense or simply think about it, it'll work just as well.

Maybe you arrive at a mix of visualising, feeling and thinking about it. Even if you are not sure what exactly you are doing but you feel good by doing it, just keep on doing it. Trust the feeling that you are doing something that is actually good for you. Your body and your feelings will guide you. If it feels good, it likely is.

When you cleanse your energy, do it responsibly. Just like you would not blow your nose into a tissue and throw the tissue down in a corridor as you walk to a colleague's office, when you do your mental cleansing, don't leave a bag of rubbish in someone else's office. When you imagine it leaving your body dispose of it responsibly. Send it to the earth with the intention of recycling it into something useful. Or burn it. Or send it up to the sky with the intention of transforming it into positive energy.

Yes, I know we are only talking about something we have made up in our minds, but please remember thoughts are actually energy. The bag of rubbish might not be a literal bag of rubbish but it will still hold the energy you just cleansed off. Whatever you do, dispose of it consciously.

If you are a spiritual or religious person, you can blend your spiritual or religious practices with your energetic cleansing. You can ask for help from the religious or spiritual entities that you pray to. You can use prayer, meditation or rituals that you are already used to.

But if you are a busy executive on your way to the next meeting and you feel, all of a sudden, your energy dropping and you have no idea what just happened, it is enough to stop for a second and notice this. Then ground. Then close your eyes, scan your energy – your body and the space just outside your body, a bubble about the size of your arms outstretched. Then pick one method, be it a shower of white light or a disk of light or a circle of fire, and pass it on through you and around you. Wash it away, burn it away, cleanse it away. Do something about it. It does not need to take a long time: it may be just a quick thought. Cleanse it away, dispose of the rubbish responsibly and then walk into your next meeting refreshed.

> *"This meeting wasn't planned!" I want to scream, but nothing comes out. Better it doesn't. He is my boss, the programme manager. I am just one of the many project managers working for him. I cannot scream at him even when he is pulling me away from my desk and into a meeting I had no idea was happening and no time to prepare for.*
>
> *"Come on, you just need to be in there for ten minutes. The top guy wants to know more about this performance indicator dashboard and asked to speak to the project manager handling this piece."*
>
> *'Oh great', I think. Ten minutes is all they need to trash my project, and me included if I don't sound convincing enough.*
>
> *"He's not in a good mood," my boss warns me. "We already talked a little bit about it and he isn't really convinced..."*

I bite my lip and still say nothing. I just feel heavy all of a sudden. A bit shaky and a bit unsure about what I am to do once I enter that meeting room where the top executives of the organisation I'm working for are having their monthly meeting. They have all the power. Including the power to fire me, a little insignificant contractor.

The meeting is on the top floor, of course it is. That's where all the top guys always live: on the top floor. I feel grateful for the few minutes of nothingness as we wait for the elevator to come.

"Don't worry, you'll be ok," my boss says encouragingly.

But his stressed voice gives a different message. And yet... they won't fire him. He is high up enough in the hierarchy not to be touched if one of the projects goes wrong. Unlike me. This is my only project and if they think they have no use for it... well, they have no use for me either.

"Ground," I think. "Just ground."

My boss is still talking but I do not hear him any longer. I start travelling down with my roots to the centre of the earth. It is a journey at lightning speed because the elevator is here and we only have a few minutes left.

By the time he presses the button for the top floor, I am already under the shower of white light. I feel my energy field, heavy and somewhat greyish; maybe I had unconsciously picked up on that conversation about my project. But I have no time to worry what this greyish thing is. I just cleanse it off.

The elevator is on the eighth floor now.

I close my eyes and for the next few seconds I totally immerse myself into the white light shower.

Bing. The doors open. I step outside and carry a bubble of light around me. I make sure it is there and I make sure I am not in my mind, trying to anticipate their questions. I have no time for that. I only have a few steps until I reach the door of that meeting room. I make sure I am in my body as I take those steps, feeling my roots and feeling the bubble of white light all around me, bathing me, making me shine.

Sparkle. Shine. White light. Roots. Safe. I am safe. Safe.

"Good morning, gentlemen," I say, smiling as I enter the meeting room. "This was unexpected but I would be happy to answer any questions you might have about my project."

The white light is still there with me as I listen to and answer their questions. I feel it: pure white light. I feel the sparkle, and I feel my energy: clean, strong and grounded.

And so is my project, they conclude after about ten minutes of questioning. Strong and grounded. In good order.

"Thank you for your time, we have no further questions."

My boss smiles relieved and nods his head. "Well done" I read on his silent lips.

The white bubble of light is still with me as I walk out of the room, back into the elevator, and as I take my place at my desk on the third floor and let out one long sigh of relief.

In addition to the ad hoc cleansing when you feel your energy has suddenly gone down, you can establish cleansing rituals. Just like you shower every morning, make it a habit to ground and cleanse your energy just after you wake up. Or do it in the evening, before you go to bed. You can do it as part of a meditation or just close your eyes and do it as you sip your cup of coffee.

The more time and attention you dedicate to it, the better it will serve you. If you make a habit of sitting still, grounding and then checking your energy to see what needs to be cleansed, you will become more accustomed to it and you will see things more clearly. Practise will make you sense more accurately where you have blockages and what exactly needs to be cleansed. You will develop your methods and you will train your mind to use them almost automatically. You will become more efficient in doing it. If you invest five minutes a day in cleansing your energy in the morning, it will pay off throughout the day in huge productivity gains.

It's important to ground before you cleanse. That way you increase your power base and use that power to cleanse. Grounding will also help you sense better what is yours and what is not, what is good for you and what you want to let go of. Grounding is an effective tool to help you boost your presence and your energy and you can use it on its own. But when you follow it by cleansing you energy, it becomes a lot more powerful. You are not only in your power base but you are cleansed of anything that holds you back.

When you practise cleansing for a while, you will become accustomed to knowing how your energy feels when it is clean and how it feels when it is not. Just like you know you need to take a shower because you have been at the gym and you smell of sweat, you will develop a sense telling you that you smell bad energetically and that you need to cleanse. Trust this feeling. Close your eyes, take your energy shower. Trust that you will feel refreshed afterwards.

Cleanse at least once a day: preferably twice a day. Cleanse after you come back home and have been on public transport. Cleanse after a particularly tough meeting. Cleanse before you go to sleep in the evening. Practise to identify and let go of what you are carrying around. Most of it is not yours anyway.

Some people are more sensitive when it comes to their energy than others, and are more impacted by the energy of others.

If you are one of them you may find that you unconsciously absorb emotions, feelings or thoughts from the people you come into contact with and end up carrying this unwanted energy with you throughout your day. You may not be aware of it, but if you practise cleansing regularly you will soon notice the difference.

Cleanse what you can and don't worry about what you can't. There's always more to it, further to go. When you hit something that simply does not want to go away, something that resists or keeps coming back, you are likely to have encountered a cord...

Energy cords and how to deal with them

A cord is a connection that forms between two entities. It can be between you and another person, a place, a pattern of thought, a job, a building, a pet, a memory or many other things. A cord is a form of energy connection.

A cord can be good for you or it can be bad. A loving cord that connects your heart to the heart of your spouse is an example of a good one. One that connects you to a person bullying you at work is an example of a bad one. Cording to memories means you keep an energy exchange open with something that resides in the past and this might stop you from directing that energy into the present. Cording to a place means you might have difficulty leaving it and when you do, it keeps calling you back.

There are many types of good cords and bad cords. Some will be easy to identify and remove if you choose to do so. Others will be a lot stronger and you might require the help of an energy worker, a healer or a psychic who can remove them for you.

Symptoms of cords

When someone links to you, they either take from your energy or send you theirs. You are likely to feel this in one or several ways:

- Your energy levels may go down. This tends to happen suddenly and if you are already in the habit of scanning your energy and knowing how you feel when you are all right, you are likely to feel the drop immediately. You may feel tired, lethargic, disoriented, irritated. You may feel you are not in the mood to do anything and you may find there is no explanation for this sudden drop. This can happen, for instance, after you have a coffee with a colleague and you suddenly feel lethargic after he's gone.

- You may find yourself riding on an emotional roller coaster. Your energy levels may go up and down, you may feel different minute by minute, hour by hour. The swings might be noticeable or subtle, but if you pay attention you will feel them. You may feel like a pendulum between two extremes, unable to understand and control the force that causes you to swing.

- You may feel a sudden and inexplicable pain somewhere in your body. It may be a pain in the ear that does not go away. I know a person who, whenever she has a pain in the ear, knows this comes from someone talking about her behind her back. Many times she found out later that it was true. Or a sudden, inexplicable muscle cramp, as if someone had just stabbed you in the back. Maybe someone actually has just done it symbolically, of course.

- Sudden, unexplained weight gain. From one day to the next you will find you have gained a few extra pounds. Of course it may just be water retention. Or the copious dinner the night before. Or anything else. It may also be a sudden influx of energy affecting you.

- A sense of loss of self; mental confusion; a feeling of uncertainty. While a day before you were quite clear about what you want to do, all of a sudden you are no longer sure, as if a haze has descended on your mind.

- Making a decision you would rather not have made and afterwards wondering "Why have I done this?" It may be that your energy was mixed up with someone else's to the point where you actually made decisions heavily influenced by someone else's energy.

- Loss of self-confidence; feeling off centre; difficulty in grounding. When you feel like you struggle to ground or find your own centre, you might be holding too many energies that are not yours. It's time for a cleanse. When you try to cleanse them but you don't feel any better, look for the cords.

- Appetite changes; different eating habits; cravings. Your body tries to deal with the energy cords in any way it can. Your energy drops so your body tries to compensate. When you feel changes in your appetite or sudden cravings, listen and ask yourself where these come from.

- Lack of sleep. This is the most common one. When people link to you with their energy and send you thoughts and feelings, you may find yourself unable to sleep, as if the activity in your energy field is suddenly intensified.

- Obsessive thoughts – you think about a person over and over again; you have mental dialogues with that person. You may think obsessively about a situation or a place or you may process endlessly a past event or conversation. No matter how much you try, you cannot stop these thoughts. Chances are you are corded to that person, place or situation.

How to cut cords

A few fortunate amongst us can actually see cords in people's auras or energy fields. They are the highly intuitive or psychic ones. They describe these cords as ropes or cables or pipes or roots or one of many other shapes and forms. They can see their colours and the point where they hook into your energy body. They can feel their texture: if they are sticky or smooth. They can see how they are attached, whether they appear to be screwed in, or hooked, or bound, or welded. They can see the energy flow in and out, and they can see the impact they have on the person who is on the receiving end of these cords.

Those of us who do not enjoy such extraordinary abilities have to make do with simply imagining them, or trying to sense them if we are inclined to sense rather than represent visually. But it works just as well. The following exercise will walk you through identifying and removing an unwanted cord.

Turn to the end of the chapter and do exercise 2.2.

After cutting a cord, give your energy time to settle. This may take a few hours or a few days. Trust that what you have done is in your best interests and give yourself time to explore this new feeling. Your energy may change. You may suddenly feel more alive, as if a draining tap is now closed. Or if you removed a cord through which another person was trying to manipulate you, your energy may feel suddenly lighter and you might feel a bit empty until your own energy levels rise to fill the space previously filled by someone else's thoughts and desires. You may feel emotionally or physically tender and tired. All these are normal symptoms after cord-cutting. Make sure you get all the rest you can, drink plenty of water, practise grounding frequently and if you can, have a salt bath or a salt scrub.

Often people you have de-corded from will show up in your life as soon as you have cut a cord. They will try to meet you, they will call you or email you. They will contact you out of the blue and they might be very insistent about seeing you. That's because at an energetic level they feel they have lost a connection with you and are keen to get it back. Be aware this is happening and handle them responsibly. It is possible to see them and interact with them and not allow them to cord back again, but you need to be aware that cording back is likely to be their conscious or unconscious desire. If you feel like waiting a few days for your energy to settle before you interact again with the people you have just de-corded, follow your gut feeling. Before you answer that call, reply to that email or agree to meet with them, ask yourself if this is good for you. If you sense it is not in your best interests but for whatever reason you have to go ahead and meet with them, take all necessary measures to protect yourself and your energy. We will cover protection techniques in the next chapter. For now, just imagining a shield of gold or silver between you and the other person as you interact with them will be enough.

If you find yourself doubting whether you are ready to let go of a person or a situation by cutting a cord, rest assured that the cords you have cut have made themselves known to you because you no longer need them. Enjoy your new energy and see where it takes you. Remember, you are on a journey to reclaim your personal power. See where this step has taken you and enjoy the extra energy that it has given you. And once you have done that, you can go further. But in order to go further you may need to overcome a few more doubts.

When the mind gets in the way

And what if it does not work? This question might have come up in your mind a few times so far. You may have chosen to read on while you feel the scepticism rising in you and the doubt growing. What if all this does not work, what if it's just a story? How do I know that grounding will increase my power? How can I prove that imagining a shower of white light cleansing my energy actually does it?

In the world of intuition there is no hard proof. The border between right and wrong is often blurred and at times confusing. There is no universal recipe. The movie that goes on inside my head might be different from yours. But the principles of energy management remain the same.

The question is not: What if all this will not work? A better question would be: Has it touched you? Has what you've read so far stirred a feeling inside you? Curiosity, perhaps, or maybe just a hope that this may actually work for you. If it has, trust that feeling. With no concrete evidence and no research to back it up, just trust it. It's yours. Whatever I write about cannot create a feeling inside you if that feeling is not yours. Go with it and see where it takes you.

It may lead you to a place between the worlds, somewhere where reason meets intuition, energy meets form… a place where the walls between the worlds are thin. Stay there for a while. Let them in, let both these worlds in as well as the inexplicable thin and moving wall that separates them. Stay there. Listen. Notice how you feel after you've done the exercises. See what happens.

What you can cleanse

First of all, start with cleansing your energy as described above. To be able to cleanse other things you need to be grounded and your energy needs to be clean.

Spaces

You can cleanse desks, rooms, buildings, your home. Do not cleanse spaces that belong to other people without their express permission. You can cleanse your space at work and your desk regularly as well as your home. Do not attempt to cleanse the whole company or department unless you are in charge of it. Cleansing the spaces around you will help keep your own energy clean. When you cleanse spaces, use the same techniques you find useful for cleansing your own energy. Disks of white light are amongst the most common but you can also use fire, water, imaginary vacuum cleaners, or anything else that might take your fancy. Always dispose of the rubbish you cleanse responsibly.

Virtual spaces

Just like you can cleanse a physical space, you can cleanse a virtual space too. Conference calls can be cleansed as a virtual meeting room, a space where participants gather to talk. Do this only if you are in charge or leading the conference call. Imagine participants arriving in a virtual meeting room and cleanse and ground that space.

Appointments in our calendar and phone calls can be cleansed in advance as well and treated as virtual meeting rooms. Simply imagine the note you made in the calendar or the space blocked for it and cleanse that. Hold the intention to cleanse any negative energy from that appointment, call or meeting as you do this.

Plans, initiatives, reports, presentations

You can cleanse any ideas or formal presentation of these ideas – plans, reports presentations, spreadsheets and so on – in the same way you cleanse your own energy or spaces. Use a disk of white light, for instance, to go through and clean all the slides of a presentation before you deliver it. Imagine the slides sparkling clean, bathed in white light afterwards. Hold the intention that all impurities, all negative energy that might have resided on those slides, is now gone. Hold the intention that anything that interferes negatively with the message presented in that report is removed and cleansed away. Pass a disk of white light through the report. Visualise it gathering all negative energies from it then dispose of it properly. For instance, imagine a fire burning the disk you used for cleansing and hold the intention that its energy gets recycled into something positive. Go back into your mind and visualise the report or presentation shining sparkling clean. You can do the same with CVs, profiles, Facebook pages, websites, a company's logo or your signature. Anything that can be visualised or imagined can be cleansed. Just remember to only cleanse what's yours or that for which you have permission to do so.

> *The puzzled voice of the high-ranking executive on the other end of the phone says it all. He does not comprehend why we are having this discussion.*
>
> *"Listen, it does not matter, does it? If the meeting comes from my calendar or your calendar, it's still the same meeting, right? Why would you want to change it over and waste so much time rebooking all these rooms in all*

these locations, making sure we have the video conference support in place? I told you I'm happy if you lead it, it's fine. You can run the meeting. I just don't see why you want to change it over to your calendar."

I can understand where he is coming from. It's difficult enough to coordinate the time of twelve participants in four different locations across three timezones. It's difficult enough to secure rooms with video connections everywhere. Once you have a series of weekly meetings set in everyone's calendars, you don't mess around with it. You just don't because life is difficult enough without trying to make it even more complicated and because everyone in this company has better things to do than booking and rebooking meeting rooms.

But he does not understand where I'm coming from. I can't tell him why, but taking this meeting over and changing it to come from my calendar is absolutely crucial for the success of this project I am supposed to lead. And no, it's not an ego boost in my role as project manager. I don't need to change it over to my calendar for that. What I need is to be able to ground and cleanse the meeting before it happens, hold the virtual space for the participants while it goes on and make sure it stays clean and grounded. And as long as the meeting invitation comes from his calendar it's based on his energy, even though he had delegated to me the responsibility of chairing the meeting. I can't ground and cleanse a meeting if the invitation comes from his calendar. I can't hold a virtual space if the meeting is based on his energy. He would have to do this. I would have to explain to him how to do it and he would have to trust me enough to try it out.

But I am not ready to talk about this yet, not to this high-flying executive at one of the top companies in the world. Not when I have been hired as a traditional project manager. Not at this point in time. Not yet.

I keep my voice steady as I tell him that I feel it is very important for the success of this project that the invitation to the weekly meeting comes from my calendar instead of his. I tell him it would give me the flexibility to control attendance, to run the meeting when he is not there. I tell him it would improve my credibility as project manager. I tell him everything I can think of as to why the meeting needs to be changed over to my calendar. I just don't mention the real reason.

In the end he agrees. I change it over and I do what I have to do. I ground it, I cleanse it. I hold the energy space for the participants. The meeting improves, the communication becomes more straightforward, the outputs more easily achieved. They soon tell me it is much better, they feel they are making progress as a team.

Every week before I chair that meeting I ground it and cleanse it. And every week, while I do this, I wonder why I didn't have the courage to tell him the real reason why I needed to take over that meeting.

When you need a little help

Body cleansing

Your energy and your body are strongly connected. If your body is clean it will impact your energy. Just taking a shower will automatically cleanse your energy to some degree. Salt is a powerful aid in cleansing, that's why a bath with added salt usually makes us feel so much more relaxed.

A thorough body detox will do even more to cleanse your energy, whatever your chosen detox method is. Many religions recommend fasting as a way to achieve a spiritual cleanse and it's all based on the connection between the state of our body and that of our energy.

Whatever your chosen method is, just keep in mind that anything you do to improve the state of your body will immediately be reflected in the state of your energy.

Spiritual practices

These include prayer, meditation, retreats, rituals, mantras or affirmations. There are many spiritual practices out there designed to help you cleanse your energy. You can pick what works for you and do it regularly if you feel this is the path for you.

Nature

Nature provides many cleansing opportunities. Just spending some time anywhere surrounded by green nature will immediately recharge our energy batteries. It is much easier to do the grounding exercises when surrounded by green nature and once the grounding is solid, any cleansing routine we use is likely to be more effective.

The sea is one of the most powerful cleansing environments; the combination of salt, water and movement make it a perfect environment to leave behind all that we no longer need. The desert with its vast open spaces, the white, snowy slopes on top of a mountain, a waterfall or the banks of a river are all powerful natural environments to assist deep cleansing moments.

Declutter

Decluttering and tiding up your physical space, your desk, your office or your home will assist with cleansing your energy as well.

Clutter holds the lower vibrational energies such as stress, depression and anxiety. Where there's clutter in your space, there will be clutter in you – either physically, mentally or emotionally. Feng shui is a traditional Chinese practice that deals with the impact the spaces around us have on the level of our energy and has a lot of recommendations around decluttering.

Plants and essential oils

Ancient civilisations often used plants to bring in peace, calm, and positivity. Native American Indians used smudging to purify or bless a place; plants such as white sage (Salvia apiana) and sagebrush (Artemisia tridentata) were used in smudging ceremonies. Smudging involves the burning of plant parts, which might not be conducive to modern-day situations. As an alternative, you can use essential oils and hydrosols to clear out negative energy and bring back positive energy.

Rose, lavender, sage and many other essences and oils are known to help assist the clearing of negative energies from our auras. A lot of literature is available on the subject and many ready-made mixtures can be purchased to help with cleansing.

Summary: How to cleanse

- ✔ Become aware of the state of your energy and when you need to cleanse
- ✔ Use one of these methods to cleanse your energy:
  - The disk of white light
  - The white light shower
  - The body scan
  - Any other visualisation that works for you.
- ✔ Establish your own regular cleansing routines.
- ✔ Identify if there are any negative cords in your energy and cut them.
- ✔ Use the same cleansing techniques to cleanse objects and concepts that are yours or that you are personally responsible for.

Cleansing Exercises

2.1 Practise cleansing your energy using your favourite visualisation technique. If one of them feels right for you, stick with it. If none of them feel right, practise adding your own elements until you become comfortable with your visualisation routine:

- Find a comfortable position: lie down, sit on a chair or sit cross-legged on a pillow on the floor.

- Ground as discussed in Chapter 1. Do that quickly. Feel your body. Focus on your breathing, formulate in your mind the intention to call your energy home and then feel your roots growing deep into the ground until they connect to the centre of the earth.

- Then pick one cleansing technique that works for you.

  The disk of white light

  ⇨ Pass a disk of white light through and around your body and see it cleansing all impurities in your energy field. Send the first one from the centre of the earth upwards into the sky and then another one from the sky to the centre of the earth. Burn it in the centre of the earth and see all the negativity it collected burning and transforming into positive energy for the earth.

  The white light shower

  ⇨ Imagine yourself under a shower of pure white light and feel how it cleanses you, how it washes away anything that you no longer need.

  ⇨ See all energy dirt going down a drain.

  ⇨ Keep the shower going until you feel light and clean.

  The body scan

  ⇨ Feel the skin on your skull. Bathe it in white light, relax it, see and feel it relaxing.

⇨ Bring your awareness to each body part in turn: your hair, your skull, your forehead, your eyes, neck, shoulders, arms, torso, belly, legs. Go down your body piece by piece and mentally relax, stretch and cleanse each part of your body using white light.

⇨ Go inside and do the same with the internal organs.

⇨ Stay with each part until you feel it relax. Try to feel each part as you visualise it and see the white light that cleanses and bathes it.

⇨ When you reach your toes, end with a quick shower of white light.

- When you feel sufficiently cleansed, ground once again, open your eyes and carry on with your day.

- Notice how you feel after each of these cleanses. What is different?

2.2 Practise identifying and cutting the cords that affect you negatively:

- Sit still on a chair or cross-legged on the floor, closer to the earth.

- Ground and cleanse as described before.

- After you finish cleansing, scan your energy and look for what's left there. Look for any cord. Hold the intention (formulate a thought in your mind) to find cords as you search all around your body.

- Pay attention to what comes to your mind as you do this. A particular person? A place? A memory? You may see something with the eyes of your imagination or you may just have a feeling or a thought, a sense of something.

- Ask to be shown whether that person, place, memory, etc. is corded to you. Go with the first image that comes to mind. Visualise the cord. Or feel it, sense it. Ask why it is there.

- The cords might be linked to a specific organ, to a chakra, to a specific part of your body or just link into your aura, the energy field all around you. Try to see or sense as much as you can about the nature and location of a particular cord.

- Sense what type of energy travels through that cord. Is it taking from your energy? Does it deliver the other person's energy to you? Their desires, their wishes, their intentions?

- Go with the first thought, the first impulse. It is usually right. Trust what comes to you no matter how hilarious or simplistic it may seem. Trust that your inner self is delivering the answer to the question you just asked.

- Ask is this good for me? Trust the answer that comes to you. Ask why it is there. What have you got to learn from it?

- Make sure you understand why and how you have allowed that person or situation to cord to you. If you are not sure, ask the question in your mind again and see what thoughts or images come to you. Forgive what you need to forgive and take responsibility for what you need to take responsibility for. Do this until you feel at peace and ready to let it go, then proceed to the next step.

- When you have understood its purpose and realise it's not good for you any longer, make a decision to remove it.

- Pull it off, cut it or imagine any other way in which you can remove it. What would you do if it was a real cord? Burn it? Cut it? Dissolve it? Use any method or any tool that comes to mind. Once you have cut the connection, pull the end of the cord from your body or energy field until there's nothing else left. Keep on pulling it, it may take a while.

- Fill the space where the cord has been removed. Infuse the hole with white or gold light. Be sure to fill the void left in the person or object that the cord was attached to as well as yourself. This ensures there is no available space for the cord to reform.

- Visualise the space that has been now completely cleansed and filled with your own energy and a healing white light. Trust that what you have done is enough.

- Pull the other end from the other person, place, memory or whatever was corded to you.

- Imagine the person or object you were corded to standing in front of you. Send them white light and let them go away. Visualise them going further and further up into the white light until they dissolve into it. When they are no longer visible, the energy link is gone.

- Go back to the cord you pulled out and make sure you have pulled every single piece of it, then dispose of it. The safest method is to burn it somewhere outside your energy field. Imagine a fire and see the cord burning, then transform the ashes into positive energy for the earth.

- Make a decision not to allow that to happen again in the future. Simply say this in your mind. It is quite common that the person who you just de-corded will sense the disconnection on some level and may respond by getting in contact. You may receive a phone call, an email or an invitation to meet. If you decide to interact with them again, maintain the firm decision that you will not allow them to re-cord to your energy.

- If they do cord again, repeat the whole process and stay away from them for a while. Trust that with any cord removal exercise you do, any potential re-cording will be weaker and weaker until eventually they will not be able to re-cord any longer.

3.

Protect: Your energy is your most valuable asset, look after it

When we leave home we lock the door. We don't leave our expensive jewellery lying around. We don't let our small kids alone in a playground. We delete spam emails and when we ride a motorbike we put a helmet on.

We do this out of a sense of self-protection. We instinctively feel responsible for protecting our bodies, our health, our families, our reputation, and our possessions.

It's the same with our energy. Just like our body or our possessions, it is vulnerable and can be harmed by others. And, just like everything else that we look after, it can be protected.

Protection comes out of a sense of self-respect, not fear. We don't think of burglars every time we lock our front door. We do this because we respect our home and its contents and we want other people to respect it too. We do this because we want to retain the right to decide which people we allow in and which people we don't. Similarly we don't think of a car crash every time we put our seatbelt on. We do it because we respect our bodies and we also do it without thinking too much. It has become an automatic routine and it's there to protect our body, just in case we need it.

Similarly, protecting our energy effectively is not done out of fear and with the worst of consequences in mind. It's grounded in self-respect and it can become an automatic routine, just like putting a seatbelt on before driving.

Protecting your energy comes naturally after grounding and cleansing and complements perfectly those routines. With practice, you will automatically ground, cleanse and protect in one go, at specific times during the day or when needed. Just as with grounding and cleansing, after an initial period of trial and experimentation, the actual routine does not need to take a long time. It only needs awareness, a few techniques and the commitment to put them into practice.

But before we talk about how to protect our energy field, let's take a look at its main gateways.

Chakras

Our bodies have seven main centres where our energy interacts with the outside world. They are known as chakras (meaning 'wheel' in Sanskrit). A lot of literature is available on this subject and it's not the purpose of this book to go into the details. But it is essential to have a basic knowledge of where they are located and the colour that corresponds to them so that we can visualise them better during our protection routines.

Our energy interacts with the outside world continuously, whether we are aware of this or not, and the bulk of this interaction happens through these chakras. When these chakras are out of balance, we will notice symptoms. When we protect our energy, we mainly work by protecting these chakras.

The illustration on the following page shows where they are, what attributes they have and what parts of the physical body they govern.

Heart Chakra

Colour: green
Location: heart
Function: centre of love, compassion, harmony, peace. Connection with the soul
Attributes: balance, acceptance, contentment, love
Physical body: lungs, heart, shoulders, arms, immune system
Symptoms of unbalance: unethical or inhuman behaviour, lack of compassion, jealousy, betrayals, inability to give or receive love, possessiveness

Solar Plexus Chakra

Colour: yellow
Location: solar plexus
Function: individuality and self worth
Attributes: emotions, joy, anger, personal power, sensitivity, ambition, image in the world, self-worth, will power
Physical body: stomach, muscles, pancreas, adrenals, liver, nervous system
Symptoms of unbalance: anger, frustration, low self-worth, lack of direction, victimisation, worry, confusion, loss of individuality

Sacral Chakra

Colour: orange
Location: lower abdomen, about two inches below the navel
Function: birth, assimilation of food, sexuality
Attributes: desire, pleasure, sexuality, procreation, creativity, relationships, change, family
Physical body: lower abdomen, kidneys, bladder, circulatory system, reproductive organs and glands, spleen, womb
Symptoms of imbalance: compulsive or obsessive behaviour, sexual dysfunctions, addictions, lack of creativity

Base Chakra

Colour: red
Location: perineum, base of your spine, behind the sacrum bone
Function: life force, vitality of physical body
Attributes: grounding, physical survival, fight or flight response, courage and patience, material success
Physical body: legs, feet, bones, large intestine, adrenal glands, immune system
Symptoms of imbalance: aggression, bullying, hyperactivity, fear, paranoia, defensiveness, procrastination

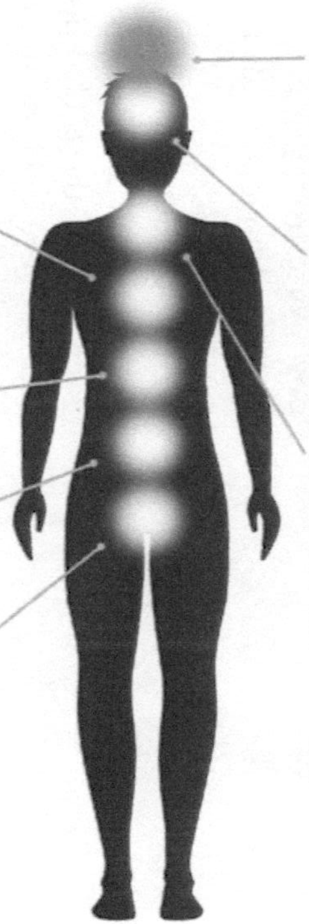

Crown Chakra

Colour: violet or white
Location: top of the head
Function: centre of spirituality
Attributes: information, understanding, acceptance, psychic skills, connection to the divine, personal purpose and destiny
Physical body: right eye, cerebral cortex, central nervous system
Symptoms of imbalance: psychological problems, mental illness, confusion, depression and despair

Brow Chakra

Colour: indigo
Location: centre of forehead slightly above eye level
Function: Centre of intuition
Attributes: perception, intuition, spirituality, wisdom, awareness, peace of mind, forgiveness
Physical body: left eye, memory, concentration, neurological function
Symptoms of imbalance: loss of memory, depression, lack of intuition, impatience, authoritarianism

Throat Chakra

Colour: blue
Location: throat
Function: centre of communication.
Attributes: creativity, self-expression, synthesising of ideas, healing, truth, transformation, reliability, kindness
Physical body: throat, neck, mouth, ears, thyroid gland
Symptoms of imbalance: inability to express oneself, dishonesty, communication problems, creativity blocks, arrogance, self-righteousness

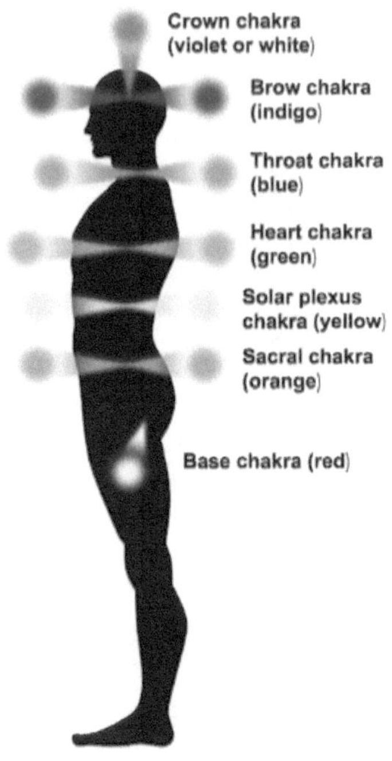

Five of the seven chakras are located on the front of the body as well as on the corresponding area at the back of the body. It is important to remember this as you visualise them. Only the crown chakra and the root chakras have no front/back correspondence. The crown chakra opens upwards from the top of our head towards the sky and the base chakra opens downward from just behind our sacral bone towards the earth.

Throughout the day and depending on the state of your energy, these chakras can be more open or more closed. The more open they are, the more they allow outside energies to connect to your energy. When you close them it's like closing the door of your home to unwanted strangers.

We are likely to open involuntarily when we are in nature, when we drink alcohol, when we take part in religious or spiritual practices, when we have a good conversation with someone, when we read a good book, see a movie we like or listen to music. Throughout the day there are many opportunities for our chakras to open up naturally and let more energy in. There's nothing wrong with this. This opening is what allows us to feel in communion with the others around us, the world, nature and our own beliefs.

The trouble starts when we forget to close them. When we take those open chakras to a meeting room full of passive-aggressive behaviour, when we meet with a colleague at work who happens to be an energy vampire, when we encounter people who try to manipulate us or to use our energy. It's like welcoming burglars into your house by leaving the door wide open.

The good news is that we can learn to close these doors and then open again when it's appropriate. And then close again. The awareness of these energetic gateways and how we can open and close them gives us enormous power and control over our own energy. The following exercise will help you practise this.

Turn to the end of the chapter and do exercise 3.1.

Opening up is usually the easy part. You will do this automatically when you meet a friend, when you spend time with your family, when you play with your dog or walk in nature. What you need to do consciously most of the time is close down.

Close down your chakras after you ground and cleanse. These activities in themselves would have opened up your energy. Close your chakras when you wake up in the morning and before you go to sleep at night. Introduce this as an automatic routine to follow your grounding and cleansing routines.

Closing down is especially important in the corporate world. Closing down your chakras will make you less prone to stress and burnout. It will stop you giving in to irrational demands and doing things you would rather not do. It will keep you safe from bullying and people trying to manipulate you. They might still try to do it but their energy will have far less impact on you compared to when you had your chakras open. Closing down your chakras consciously is one of the most powerful things you can do for yourself. You are basically denying access to anyone harmful. You are taking charge of your own energy. You are maintaining and increasing your power.

Connecting and disconnecting

You can also use your chakras to connect and disconnect from people, places, ideas or situations. Just remember that when you connect, always to do it from your heart chakra to their heart chakra and maintain an honest intention in your mind to do that for the greatest benefit of all parties. Never connect from another chakra or to people's other chakras, since you may impact both their energy and yours in a negative way. Exceptions to this rule are that lovers will automatically be connected both at the heart and at the sacral chakras and young children will be connected to the base chakra of their mother.

For the purpose of maintaining your energy integrity in the corporate world, remember to only connect at heart level, for a specific purpose, and disconnect afterwards. For instance, in the corporate world, you may want to connect to your co-workers for a team-building event or for a meeting. You may want to connect to a colleague as you prepare for an important conversation, or to the audience before you give a presentation. This energy connection will significantly improve the quality of the interaction you have, the connection your audience feels with you during a presentation or the output of a teamwork exercise. But remember, just as you connect, it is important to disconnect afterwards.

The following exercise will help you connect and disconnect consciously.

Turn to the end of the chapter and do exercise 3.2.

Protection routines

Just as you can connect and disconnect from other people, they can do the same to you, either consciously or unconsciously. Some of these connections will be good for you and will be done with the best of intentions. This is the case of loving connections with friends and family members, when you feel supported, valued and loved. You can also have positive connections to people or groups you barely know but that you feel 'on the same wavelength' as. Some connections, though, might be bad for your energy levels and as a result you may feel depleted, manipulated or even attacked.

If we think of the energy field around our body as part of us, we can protect it just as we protect our body. But how can we do this? It is easy to put on a helmet when we ride a motorbike to protect our skull in case of an accident. Or a seatbelt as we drive. Well, we can do the same for your energy. The only difference is that we will have to imagine it.

But what do we protect our energy from? We protect it from any negative impact it may receive. This can come from other people's energy that might have entered our energy field, their moods, emotions, thoughts and intentions even when they have nothing to do with us. Or it can come from cords other people might have sent us. Or from being drained by an energy vampire. Or from any form of low energy that might be present in a space. In extreme cases we can also protect from psychic attack, as described later in this chapter.

There are many types of protection techniques and the list below is just for your reference. As with everything that has to do with your energy, it is important for you to find your own way to do it. Experiment with some of the ideas below and see what works for you and what doesn't. If you come up with a different symbol or visualisation that works better for you, that's perfect. Just use that.

All methods below can be added to your routines for grounding, cleansing and closing your chakras. And with all these methods, the most important thing is to hold the intention to protect yourself and to believe that whatever you have done works for you.

Protective cloak

Imagine being dressed in a long cloak of protective light. It can be any colour you choose. Envision it covering your arms and its hood covering your head. Imagine the hem of the cloak touching the earth. Feel the material on your skin. Feel it moving as you move. Feel its weight on your shoulders. Know that it will protect you from any unwanted energies.

Gold edge around your aura

Imagine your energy field all around you as a bubble of white light about the size of your outstretched arms around your body. See the edges of this bubble coated in thick layers of gold. See this layer as strong and impenetrable. See it shining. See it reflecting back into the universe any unwanted energies that come towards you. As you see this, form the intention that any unwanted energies reflected back into the universe are changed into positive energy. This is because we don't want to send anything bad into the world even if this is a simple reflection of what came to us.

Armours, shields, helmets

These are variations of the cloak method described above. You can dress yourself in imaginary armours, hold shields, put on a helmet, or a protective overall, whatever takes your fancy. If you can visualise it, just do that. If you find it difficult, try to sense it. If you are not sure you can either sense or visualise it, just think about it.

Mirrors

These can be used as a variation of the shield of gold described above or as a top-up. You can imagine the edge of your aura made of mirrors, reflecting the energy that comes to you back into the universe. Hold the intention to reflect back anything that is negative for you and change it into positive energy as it gets reflected. Don't worry about how this is done. Just keep this thought in your mind. Also hold the intention that anything that is positive for you will find its way to you.

Bubble of white light

Imagine this all around you and imagine it keeps you clean and protected. This is useful especially when you have to interact with energy vampires, as described further in this chapter. Imagine the other person also in their own bubble of white light and see the clear demarcation between your bubbles. Keep them separate. If you feel like it, you may add another layer of colour on top of your bubble of white light. Do so especially if you feel attracted to a specific colour. If it comes to your mind it means your energy needs the vibration of that colour at that particular moment in time.

The most important thing with all these methods is your firm intention to protect yourself from any kind of negative energy, from wherever it may come and in whatever way it may show up. Hold this thought as you pick your method and as you develop your own. Remember that energy follows thought so just maintaining this intention in your mind will be enough to deliver a layer of protection to your energy field.

Our auras, the energy fields all around us, will give us naturally a certain degree of protection from these negative intrusions. But sometimes our auras get weakened. Lack of sleep, negative emotions, sickness, stress, alcohol, pollution, drugs and medicines can weaken our energy fields and inevitably our level of protection. While a light top-up will be enough when your aura is strong and clear, you may find that you need to do a lot more when you feel depleted. Follow your impulse as you imagine your chosen method of protection.

Protect your energy on a daily basis as a routine practice and top up your protection when you feel the need to. Gradually your energy will become stronger and you will need less intense visualisation to achieve a comfortable level of protection.

Energy loss and why it happens

There are many types of energy loss and various situations that cause them. They vary in the strength of the impact they have on us. In some situations it's enough to ground, cleanse and protect. For others, we might need some specialised help.

We may be losing energy because this is how we have been accustomed to function. We may even not be aware that we are doing so on a regular basis and we may function like a water tap left on. Once we realise this and we turn off that tap, we might be amazed to see what a difference that makes to our overall sense of well-being, vitality and capacity to manifest the life we want.

Let's take a look at the most common types of energy drainages:

Thoughts and emotions

A thought is a form of energy. It forms in someone's mind and it's directed at something. If that something or someone is you, it will travel towards your energy, and depending on the state you are in and the intensity of the thought, it may impact you. These thoughts are often based on emotions and the lower the vibration of the emotion (like depression, anger, rage, jealousy, fear), the more destructive the energy of the thought directed towards you.

When thoughts are repeated often enough, they become thought forms. These can be the repetitive thoughts of other people that have travelled to your energy and are sitting there in your energy field. Or they can be the expectations these people have of you, things they hope you do or don't do, or they can be destructive thoughts based on the low vibrational emotions mentioned above. Or they can be your own destructive thought patterns that, through repetition, have started to hold a permanent place in your energy field.

Let's take a look at how a low vibration emotion like envy can impact upon you.

Let's say you just started a new relationship and are happily talking about how great you feel. Your single friend might send you envy. You get promoted at work and are congratulated by your colleagues. Likely many of those congratulating you will send you conscious or unconscious envy. You get married and have a wonderful wedding reception with a lot of guests. Many of those guests who are not in a state of similar bliss will send you envy. Envy is so common these days that it has become perfectly socially acceptable to say "I'm so jealous" when you tell others about the holidays you have had, the car you have bought or the person you have fallen in love with. And in the corporate world, and especially in those working cultures where people compete with each other heavily for promotions, rewards or power, envy is at every corner.

Envy comes from people who are not solidly anchored in their power base. Often they are sad, unhappy, disillusioned and feeling low. They feel powerless to get what they want. So they try to take some of your power. Envy is an attempt to take your energy. They don't really want your holiday, your promotion, your car, your job or your house. What they want is the energy increase they think these things have brought to you. They want to enjoy that feeling; they are hungry for that energy. What they absolutely don't want and don't think about is the effort it took you to get there. They don't want the work, the uncertainty, the decisions you had to take or the things you had to give up to be able to get there. When you talk about your holidays, no one wants to hear how much you paid and what sacrifices you had to make to be able to save that money. This is not on people's agendas. All they want is the final product; they want to be you at that specific point in time. They want the energy load that comes to you from that particular achievement, recognition or fulfilment. To put it simply, they want your energy.

You open yourself up to envy by leaving a piece of your energy with the people who envy you. By trying to see yourself through their eyes. If your sense of self is not sufficiently anchored into your power base, you may try to subconsciously see yourself through the eyes of other people just to reinforce that you have indeed done well. You may, consciously or not, try to impress them. This opens you up to their envy, to this form of energy robbery.

I am not saying that you should not celebrate your successes. On the contrary, celebrating and sharing successes reinforces them and the energy you get from these accomplishments. Go ahead and celebrate, talk about them. But do this from a place of inner strength, with all your energy called inside your body and grounded, do this protected and stay alert for and aware of any form of envy that might enter your field. Clean that off. Cut negative cords. Stay inside your energy field, don't try to see yourself through the eyes of others, don't try to impress, to get energy from their admiration or approval. Stay in your energy, stay in your power. If you are there, you will not be touched by their envy.

At work, make sure your energy is grounded, cleansed and protected before you start your day. Check the status of your energy throughout the day and be aware when that changes. If you feel something has entered your field, clean it away as soon as you can before it has time to stick.

Manipulation attempts are based on thoughts as well. People try to make you do or not do certain things. They think about this intensively. They even try to stir emotions in you to accomplish this, perhaps by making you feel guilty or fearful. Again, once your energy is grounded, cleansed and protected, their attempts will not reach you. If they do, if you feel suddenly affected by what someone else wants you to do, become aware and cleanse that energy away. Then protect your energy once more.

When you do this regularly, something happens. People around you start to perceive that it's not easy to mess with your energy. They may attempt to manipulate you a few times, but when they see it does not work they will usually give up. Also, you may find that gradually you surround yourself with healthier people. Once you maintain and increase your level of energy, it will attract similar, cleaner energies around it.

The following exercise will help you identify and remove negative thought forms from your energy field.

Turn to the end of the chapter and do exercise 3.3.

Energy vampires and how to protect from them

The energy vampires, also called psychic vampires, are a common creature of the corporate corridors. They look like you and me, they talk normally, they come across as nice people, competent and even empathetic. They are keen to help others. Maybe a little bit too keen. They often give an impression of success, excitement and charisma. We often like them at first sight. This is exactly what they need. They need people to like them because when we like someone we consciously or unconsciously open up to them. And then it becomes easy for them to do what they do habitually: feed off our energy.

Vampires do not only belong to movies. They are quite real and you are likely to have met a few in your working life already.

She may be the co-worker who often comes to your desk to pick your brain on a specific subject. Or the colleague who always sends you messages with no clear purpose, just to keep in touch. Or the boss who tries to micromanage you. Or the other colleague who always comes to share gossip with you. Or the friend who always gets herself into trouble and needs a sympathetic ear. They have one thing in common: they want your energy.

Vampires act normally. They are people like you and me. They are people who are not able to get their own energy from the infinite pool naturally available to us all. They have trouble connecting to the life force all around them. They have learned to get energy from other people and they carry on doing this, consciously or unconsciously. Under one condition though: if we allow it. Someone else can only feed off our energy if we allow it, either knowingly or not.

They will gain your attention, your friendship and your sympathy. They will make you care for them. They will pose as friends. They will try to be helpful. They might be your bosses, teachers or mentors and may look like they are helping you. Once they gain your goodwill, you will start opening up to them and slowly they will start drawing energy from you. You may feel that as a slight draining at first. You have a coffee with a colleague in a lunch break and they tell you all about a personal or a professional difficulty. You feel for them. You try to empathise with them. Maybe you try to offer possible solutions. Usually your practical ideas will get rejected and the vampire will go on and on about their issues and problems and you will carry on listening to them. At the end of the twenty minutes you are left drained of energy and as you walk back to your desk you are not quite sure what happened.

Or they might give you a call. They might try to pick your brain on a new idea. You listen to them, you give them honest feedback. You genuinely want them to succeed. You give them your attention and energy. Very little comes back from them but you don't mind this at first. And yet, when you put down the phone, you feel tired.

Some energy vampires will be control freaks or micromanagers. They will take pleasure in controlling every single detail of the work of the people reporting to them. They use this as a way to tap into the energy of these people. Some others will draw energy simply by contact; they are usually the ones that want to talk a lot, to catch up frequently. They need human interaction to fill their energy reservoirs.

Some need conflict. They will create a state of anger and aggression around them so that people become intimidated or fearful. Once you are in that state, your energy becomes vulnerable and you will be an easier prey. This type of vampire feeds on the fear and anxiety they create in the people around them.

Some need your pity. They have not developed their internal power sufficiently to sort out their own issues and they lack the courage to face them. All they want is someone else's pity as a form of energy substitute that will allow them to carry on with whatever situation they are facing without the need to actually do anything about it.

Yet others are charismatic individuals who project around them a sense of success and power. A closer look, however, makes it clear that the success is not accompanied by inner peace, nor the power by a strong foundation. They walk around as inflated egos and need other people to admire them so as to maintain the bubble that protects their fragile egos. These people need your admiration. They are the ones taking thousand of selfies on holidays and posting them on Facebook. Look at me, admire me. Give me your attention, your admiration. Since energy follows thought, once you give them your attention you will in fact give them your energy.

Vampires are all around us and most of them are unconscious of what they do. They don't see their abyss of need that makes them cling to and drain energy from another human being. Most of the time, the victims of the vampires are similarly unconscious. You may not be aware that you have been tricked into opening up your energy to the vampire. But once you become conscious you can easily stop it. And once you stop the supply, the vampire will cut the connection and drop off you like a tick that cannot suck blood any more.

But how do we recognise them? How do we know when we are dealing with a vampire and when we are dealing with a friend in genuine need of someone to empathise with their situation? Does chasing vampires from our lives turn us into uncaring, egotistical and unempathetic creatures?

The difference lies in how you feel. If you ask the question, your inner barometers will tell you if that connection is good or bad for you. If you feel drained after speaking to someone on the phone, pay attention to that feeling. See if you get it again the next time you interact with the same person. If you feel fine and full of energy even after you had a dinner with a friend and talked about their problems, pay attention to that feeling. It tells you your energy is fine in the company of that person.

You can still be a caring person and offer a sympathetic shoulder to your friends or family. You can still genuinely help out a colleague at work. You can still admire someone and want to be like them. All these interactions do not necessarily mean you are losing energy. On the contrary, you can exchange energy with someone and at the end of that exchange you can both feel better and healthier for it. The main difference in these situations is that there is an exchange of energies rather than a taking of yours. You might listen to a friend's issues and feel that person respecting your energy boundaries. You will usually feel a sense of balance when you do this. You know your friend will be there for you on similar occasions. Vampires don't reciprocate.

It really is as simple as that. Our awareness of our energy holds the key here. Pay attention to how you feel and you will find out when you are interacting with a vampire.

How do you stop the supply of energy? Firstly, become aware of who they are and what the interaction with them does to your overall feeling of well-being. Notice what happens to your energy levels. When we know we are dealing with an energy vampire who has been feeding off our energy, often the hardest thing to do is to accept that we have let that happen, that we have turned on the tap.

Just as you turned it on you can turn it off. When you interact with them next, make sure your chakras are closed as described in the exercise above. Imagine each of your seven chakras closed off with a door and a lock. Make sure you put a bubble of white light around you to protect your energy. Imagine a bubble of white light around them as well. Or picture a wall between you and the other person.

Stay inside your white light and don't go out energetically towards the vampire no matter how inviting they feel. Keep a check on your sense of caring, of pity, on your feeling that you should do more to help. Keep a check on the feeling of guilt they will try to stir inside you. Keep a check on your taps and visualise them turned off at all times.

See what happens to the interaction when you are in that state. The healthy connections will survive this. You can still interact with a genuine friend with your chakras closed and it will be fine. An energy vampire will become frustrated though. They will feel the energy supply is turned off. They will get angry, they will confront you, they will try to make you feel bad. They will call you egotistical, uncaring. They will try to do anything they can to make you turn on the tap again.

A genuine friendship survives long periods of noninteraction just fine. You might have friends you have not seen in years and when you meet them again, nothing has changed. It feels like you saw them yesterday. This is not possible with an energy vampire. As soon as they feel the energy supply is off, they will go in search of it elsewhere. If a friend deserts you after you have been unavailable energy-wise for them, rest assured you have not lost anything. It likely was an energy vampire who has cut a connection that's gone dry.

On the other hand, if you have difficulties maintaining the closed energy state when around them and it's clear to you that this person is feeding off your energy, cut the connection yourself. Then stay away from them for a while. You may find that feelings of guilt arise in you as you do this. This is part of the conditioning the vampire has created to make you stay open. Resist this guilt. Accept what you are feeling but keep your commitment to protecting your own energy. The following exercise will help you practise identifying and cutting off from energy vampires.

Turn to the end of the chapter and do exercise 3.4.

Psychic Attack

A psychic attack is not that common but when it happens you are guaranteed to feel it. The symptoms will be strong, they will feel very intense. You are likely to be affected physically, not just emotionally. In some extreme cases you will not be able to sleep, eat or function properly.

Psychic attacks happens when someone with powerful energy sends you intense prolonged negative energy (like thoughts, for instance), or hires someone skilled at these practices to do so. This is usually the area where black magic, voodoo and other similar practices operate. But not necessarily. Sometimes attacks may come from someone in your work environment, from an ex-lover or from within your own family.

Someone in a corporate environment can send you intense negative energy for a prolonged time simply because they want your job or because they feel you are stopping their success. Whatever the reason and wherever it may come from, you are likely to feel the negative impact and when you do, you will have to take action to protect yourself.

The risk is that you start doubting what you feel and talk yourself out of it. You tell yourself that you are exaggerating, that what you feel is not really there. That it can't be that bad. You tell yourself you can handle this.

When you feel there is something powerful messing with your energy, something that does not go away when you try to ground, cleanse and protect, it's time to ask for help. There are many energy practitioners out there, reiki masters, healers, shamans and so on, who will be able to do this energy work for you.

Whatever you do, don't ignore it hoping it will go away by itself. It likely won't. Just take it seriously and do something about it. Also, never retaliate; never send bad thoughts back to someone as a way of protecting yourself. This will only serve to create further trouble as everything we send into the world eventually comes back to us.

Here are some possible signs of a psychic attack. As with every symptom, they can mean a lot of different things, signify a medical condition or simply be coincidences. Use this list as a reminder, but most importantly trust your own intuition.

- Feeling drained, low energy
- Obsessive thoughts and/or images
- Recurring nightmares
- Major changes in behaviour for no reason
- Sudden, irrational fears
- Sensing a presence as if you are being watched
- Unexplained pains anywhere in the body
- Sudden illness that resists any diagnostic attempt
- Strange, recurring accidents
- Other people's anger directed towards you for no reason
- Visions or hallucinations

If you feel there's something going on but are not sure what it is, just ask a qualified professional to check. Better safe than sorry.

Also, you may think that once you know what is going on and from whom it comes, you could simply confront the situation in the real world. This can work only if the energetic load is cleared first. If you are still under psychic attack, the actions you take in the real world might not be enough or you might not be able to take them.

For a few days I've been feeling like I am slowly losing my mind. All I can think about is this woman, a work colleague of mine. Her face is following me as I close my eyes at night but I cannot sleep. I am talking to her. In my mind I am constantly talking to her. I am defending myself. I am explaining things. I am arguing with her. I am talking about her to others as well. I do this in my mind most of the time but I talk about her in my real life too. I mention her when people ask me how my job is going. I mention her with a mixture of rage and irritation. I tell people again and again what is happening between her and me, the irritation, the backstabbing I feel, the jealousy I perceive in her. I know they don't really care but I simply cannot stop talking about her.

Every night before I go to sleep I rehearse what I am going to do the next day if I interact with her again. How I am going to respond to one of her nasty emails. How I am going to take it if she suddenly turns around and stabs me in the back in the middle of a meeting in front of other people, as she so often does. I am planning my response. I am planning my moves.

But it all fails. This woman is simply bullying me, and she is in a position of power and I am not. No matter how much I defend myself she is coming for me, day after day. I know it's not personal. She just wants my job and she had probably thought that I, a newcomer, wouldn't last long anyway. But I did. She did not like this and started her attacks.

I am holding on and carrying on with my work, hoping it will stop. But it does not. Instead it gets worse. For a few days now I haven't been able to sleep at night because I am lost in the conversations I hold with her in my mind.

I know it's pointless to confront her. I have spoken to my boss about this but the politics of this company are such that he cannot do too much. Nor does he actually care, in the big scheme of things my little struggle with that woman does not matter. I am left alone, day after day, to deal with the obsessive thoughts I have about this woman.

Actually, what she does in real life is not that bad: a sharp email; a meeting taken over; a refusal to cooperate on a project. Things that sometimes happen in the corporate world and one has to brush over. No, that is not what keeps me awake at night.

The real problem is that somehow she has got into my brain. She lives there and destroys my health and my peace whether I am at home or in the office. Whatever I do, I cannot keep my mind off her. I am afraid I'm going insane.

The situation goes on until one day I ask for help. No, not from my boss. Not from the HR department. I go to a healer. I tell her I cannot live like this any longer. She tells me she can sense this person in my aura, that I am not crazy. She tells me she believes me when I say I feel like I am losing my mind. Then she tells me she will remove this woman's energy from my own. I don't know what she does next and how she does it, but when I get home that day I realise the face of that woman is no longer with me.

And then I finally find the strength to do what I should have done a long time before. I go to work the next day and I write a long email to her and to a lot of others connected with our projects. I say I want to clear off any possible confusion about roles and responsibilities. I state my understanding of how things are supposed to work. I ask them to let me know if they think differently. I press send. For a few days I fear they will fire me for this. It was a risky gamble and it upset a lot of powerful people.

But they don't. They decide to accept it instead. Nobody challenges it, nobody puts on paper a different version of reality. And from that moment on she never bothers me again.

Over-protection and under-protection

When you start your regular protection routine you are likely to start from a habitual place of under-protection. While we regularly get bombarded with messages about being open, empathetic, selfless and caring, we're not really taught to be protected and closed towards other people or situations. Hence we are likely to walk around with our energy open. Depending on how energy-sensitive we are, we become drained sooner or later.

When we learn to protect our energy, we realise how much of it we have lost in the past. All of a sudden, we understand who the people who were taking it are. It can be quite a shocking realisation but once we allow ourselves to see the truth we are likely to remember it.

As we start closing down and drifting away from people who were previously feeding from our energy, we might get accused of becoming selfish, too closed up, too self-obsessed. Some of this will just be forms of emotional blackmail from people who want to regain the free access to our energy they enjoyed before. But on other occasions this might be a real risk. There is a danger that we become too locked off, too self-absorbed, too protective of our energy. There is a chance that other people who genuinely want to connect with us won't be able to do so because of the thick layers of protection we have placed around us. Over-protection might also make us miss opportunities or stop us from attracting the things that we want in our lives.

So between under-protection and over-protection, where is the right balance?

As with every piece of energy work, there is no right or wrong answer. When we initiate a change we are likely to overdo it at first, jump from too little protection to too much protection. This is normal and it's part of the journey of any transformation. Don't be scared of it. Let yourself experiment. Let yourself feel what is right for you. If you start off with too much protection, you can relax that gradually and see if that serves you well. If people accuse you of being uncaring and insensitive, hold on for a while before relaxing your protection. Wait to see and feel if they are genuine or if this is just a form of manipulation. Take it easy, experiment and see where it gets you. Remember that it's your energy you are protecting and you have every right in the world to do so.

However, there is one clear indicator that can show you if you are over-protecting: the sensation of fear. Are you doing it out of fear?

Fear is a low vibration energy and will automatically lower your protection. No matter how many shields you place around you, how many cloaks of protection you put on, if you do this based on fear you will lower the protection you are trying to create for yourself. You will unconsciously perceive that your protection layer is not strong enough and you will do more and more and likely end up over-protected. And yet that protection might not be effective.

Bear that in mind as you start experimenting with protection techniques and ask yourself that question every time you do it. If you sense you are doing it out of fear, refocus your emotions towards self-respect. Feel your connection to your body. Ground your energy. Turn your attention inside and get in contact with your energy, your personal power. Feel your respect and love for that energy. Focus on this, focus towards, not against. Towards your energy, not against the bad things trying to get to you. Changing the perspective always helps.

What if the aggressor was you?

All this works well when you protect your energy from someone else's negative interference. But there's one more thing we need to be aware of: sometimes we are the aggressors.

It's hard to accept that you have done or can do to other people exactly what you are trying to protect yourself from. Assuming you are an ethical person and mean to do well, it can come as a shock that sometimes you might be interfering with the energy of other people unconsciously in a way that is having negative effects on them.

You might have envied them. You might have tried to influence them to do or not to do something that you wanted. You might have desperately wanted someone to fall in love with you. You might have sent them negative thoughts in a rage. You might have wished them ill as a form of revenge.

We are all humans and, as such, imperfect. We might have done things we regret. The good news is that as soon as you become aware of it, you can repair it.

If the harm was done via energy, the repair needs to be done via energy as well. Let's say you got angry with someone in your mind and had bad thoughts about that person. As a form of energy, your bad thoughts are likely to have travelled to that person. Once you become aware of this you might be tempted to connect to them in the real world, explain things and ask for their forgiveness. This likely won't work. Not to mention the weirdness of the situation, even if they say they forgive you, the energy load of the thoughts you sent them might still stay with them.

So what do you do? You take them back – your thoughts, I mean. You call your energy home. You close your eyes, you ground, cleanse, protect your energy and then call back and neutralise any negative thoughts you might have sent the other person. You check for any cords you might have sent to them and you take those back too. You call them all back and you imagine burning them or dissolving them. You make sure you get back every single piece of your energy from that person.

Then you send them white healing light and ask for their forgiveness in your own mind.

"I should be able to do this," I tell myself. "I should be able to clear and protect my energy." I know I should. By now I know enough to be able to do this. But somehow I can't this time; it's too strong. I hate him with an intensity that originates somewhere deep inside my guts, raises up through my chest and explodes into my head. I hate this man so much that if he were close to me right now I would gouge his eyes out.

I am surprised at the intensity of my own feelings. After all, he did not do anything too bad, he only attempted to micromanage me. He is just a little control freak, an occasional energy vampire. I have worked with others like him and some of them were a lot worse. He only tried to harass me with some emails and phone calls.

But no, this is not the issue. I am not quite sure what the issue actually is. I am not sure what is happening. I am sitting down and trying to meditate in the morning before I go to work and his face flashes in front of my closed eyes. The feeling of anger flares up again, intense, burning my insides.

After a few useless attempts to ground, clear and protect, I give up. I call a good friend who is accustomed to energy work and uses all these methods as well. I ask for her help.

She grounds, cleanses and protects her own energy first. She then starts meditating. In her own mind she asks to be shown what is happening with my energy. She spends a few minutes visualising this then she calls me back.

"His energy was all around your head. I could see cords into your brain, everywhere. I have removed them. I think you should feel better now."

I know enough to understand this is a form of psychic attack strong enough to disable my own power to protect myself. As my friend is external to this situation, the energy attack on me did not have an effect on her. Once she has removed the cords, I can ground, cleanse and protect my own energy. I cleanse every little piece of his energy from my field, all his needs and wants that have created the blockages I felt.

But I do not stop here. The rage in me is still bubbling and I go out to get him. I am angry at his energy aggression and I want to punish him. In my mind, after I cleanse and protect my aura I go after him. I want to teach him a lesson he will never forget. I want to teach him to stay away from me and the anger I feel inside is my engine.

I lose myself in my revenge fantasies, sending him the same aggression I feel he sent to me.

I carry on doing this until I hear a voice in my mind. "Stop," it says. It is so clear, so powerful, that I can't ignore it. I have no idea where it is coming from but I can't ignore it.

And then I realise what I have been doing. In response to his aggression, I am now attacking him myself.

I stop. I take a deep breath. I call my energy home. I watch it returning. It takes a while, since I have sent a lot of it to him. I take it back, every little single piece of it. I imagine cleansing and burning off the angry thoughts. Then I send him a healing white light in my mind and see it bathing and healing him. The feeling of anger is gone. In my mind, I tell him I am sorry. I keep on sending him white light for a few days whenever I think about him. And I keep on doing that long after he stops trying to micromanage me, that very same week.

We are all human and we all make mistakes. When you discover one, don't panic. Just correct it. The following exercise will show you how to deal with it.

Turn to the end of the chapter and do exercise 3.5.

What you can protect

Your energy is the most important asset you have and should be your top focus for protection. In addition, any object or concept that can be grounded and cleansed can be protected as well.

Spaces

You can protect your home, your desk, your office and any space that is yours and that you have grounded and cleansed first. Imagine a bubble of white light around anything you want to protect, or use any other form of visualisation you feel attracted to.

Plans, initiatives, reports, presentations

As with grounding and cleansing, you can use protection on a variety of outputs. Plans, initiatives, reports, presentations, calls: all of these can benefit from a layer of protection after grounding and cleansing. Your professional reputation can be visualised and protected, as can your Facebook or LinkedIn page, your business cards or your logo. Anything that you can visualise a white bubble of light around, can be protected. Hold this intention in your mind as you visualise the object or the concept. Be creative with non-form concepts. Your professional reputation can be imagined as your business card or as your LinkedIn profile. Do this whenever you feel the need to but don't become obsessed by it. Trust that the protection you have imagined in your mind is actually working in reality.

Emails

Emails are the core of our corporate life. Emails are written thoughts and as such they are a form of energy. They can be protected as well as sent out with the best intention. Always add a layer of light and an intention that the email will do its job in the best possible way before you press send, particularly for tricky or controversial emails. Protect them in a bubble of white light. Set a good intention.

When you need a little help

Like grounding and cleansing, protection is made with your own intention and with the help of visualisation. There are things, however, you can use when you feel like you need some help. The list below is not exhaustive, it only aims to offer some suggestions.

Crystals and gemstones

Black obsidian and black tourmaline are known to increase protection. You can place a crystal on your desk, carry one in your handbag or in your pocket. Alternatively you can find jewellery made of these crystals. Pendants worn over the thymus gland are particularly effective.

Spiritual and religious symbols

According to your beliefs, there are numerous spiritual or religious symbols you can use for protection or entities you can pray to and ask for their help. Symbols like the Cross, the Star of David, the Tree of Life, Merkabah and the Hand of Fatima are worn for protection by millions of people. Whatever your belief, remember that your innermost conviction is the most important thing here. The power of prayer lies with the person who is praying and his own conviction that his prayer will be heard.

Aromatherapy

Normal incense or Tibetan incense are known for the property of dissolving negative energies. Some essential oils are also helpful for energy protection: rose, basil, lavender, juniper and peppermint, amongst others.

Mantras and affirmations

They work when done with the intention of protection and added to your routine. Words are a form of thought and thought is energy, hence words, even if you only speak them in your mind, have a powerful energy load. Spoken out loud, their effect intensifies.

Many cultures believe that words have supernatural constructive powers and modern psychology has incorporated the belief that the language we use has the power to subconsciously shape our life. If you tell yourself you will not be able to do something, you are in fact diminishing the very energy you need in order to accomplish that thing. Equally, if you tell yourself that you are feeling good, chances are you are going to actually feel better.

Summary: How to protect

- ✔ Make sure you are connected to your power base, that you are grounded and inside your body. This is the most basic form of energy protection.

- ✔ Learn where your chakras are and the type of energy they represent.

- ✔ Practise opening and closing them consciously.

- ✔ Practise connecting and disconnecting from other people.

- ✔ Choose a protection technique and make it a regular routine.

- ✔ Be aware of the possible negative influence of other people's energy and learn to protect against it.

- ✔ Learn to recognise and protect yourself from energy vampires.

- ✔ Ask for help if you are under psychic attack.

- ✔ Find your optimum level of protection and stick to it.

- ✔ Clear any negative energy you might have sent to other people.

- ✔ Add a protection technique to your grounding and cleansing routines for yourself, your spaces, your objects and your concepts.

Protection Exercises

3.1 Practise opening and closing your chakras consciously:

Opening your chakras:

- Sit comfortably on a chair or cross-legged on the floor.

- Ground and cleanse your energy, as explained in previous chapters.

- Bring your attention to your root chakra and imagine it opening so that red energy travels down to the centre of the earth. Breathe in and out three times, expanding your root energy with every breath.

- Bring your attention to your sacral chakra and imagine it opening out in front of you and behind you. Breathe in and out three times, expanding your sacral energy with every breath.

- Repeat for solar plexus, heart, throat and brow chakras.

- Bring your attention to your crown chakra and imagine it sending white energy that travels up to the highest point of light you can imagine. Breathe in and out three times, expanding your crown energy with every breath.

- Do these steps both for the front and back of the body for all the chakras except for the crown and the root chakra. The root chakra opens downwards towards the earth and the crown chakra opens upwards towards the sky.

- Ask for protection. If you have spiritual or religious beliefs, use any religious entity, guides, angels or power animals you feel comfortable with. If not, form an intention in your mind (a thought) that your energy is protected.

- You are now open.

Closing your chakras:

- Start with the crown chakra and work your way downwards.

- Draw in the bright, coloured energy of each of the chakras and imagine it going inside your body until there's nothing left outside.

- Then imagine a door closing the entrance of each of the chakras.

- For the solar plexus, imagine a door closing and lock it three times. Put a padlock on it. Add a protective disk of golden light in front of the door for extra protection. This is because the solar plexus chakra is the most common chakra to which people tend to cord.

- For all the chakras except for the crown and the base chakra, do this visualisation both for the front and back of the body.

- For the base chakra, draw the door in but do not close it completely: leave a tiny ray of red light going down towards the centre of the earth together with your roots. Protect this ray of red light in a layer of white light and leave it connecting you to the centre of the earth. This ensures you stay grounded.

- Once you finish with all the chakras, check your roots are in the ground. Readjust them if they have moved.

- Open your eyes and take a deep breath.

- You are now closed. This automatically offers you a degree of protection.

Addressing imbalances of chakras:

Just practising opening and closing your chakras will improve the flow of energy going through each of them. To further address imbalances, imagine cleansing each chakra with white light until you can visualise the flow of light in the corresponding colour emanating from each chakra clear and strong.

More in-depth chakra balancing can be carried out by energy practitioners, healers or shamans.

> **3.2 Practise connecting and disconnecting to participants before a conference call.**

Connecting:

- Sit comfortably on a chair.

- Feel the soles of your feet on the floor. Ground and cleanse.

- Send a beam of white light from your heart to the hearts of all the participants in that conference call.

- Hold the intention that this connection is made in honesty, for the greatest good of everyone and for the duration of that conference call only.

- You are now connected to them.

Disconnecting:

- Imagine the cord linking your heart to the heart of each of the participants dissolving.

- Hold the intention that each of you is now free to go on with their day.

- Check your roots into the ground. If they have moved, readjust them.

- Cleanse your energy if the meeting was particularly heavy or aggressive.

- You are now disconnected.

> **3.3 Practise identifying and removing negative thought forms from your energy:**

- Ground and cleanse as described in Chapters 1 and 2.

- Imagine a disk of white light descending over your body and your aura, which is the space around your body about the size of your outstretched arms.

- Hold the intention that this disk specifically gathers all negative thought forms.

- Pass it slowly from your head to your toes, through your body and through the space around you.

- Visualise what it gathers in whatever form it may come to your mind.

- Take the disk and whatever it gathers deep into the earth, where you build a big fire and burn it. See it burning until there's nothing left of it.

- Continue with a routine to protect your energy. Use shields, white lights, bubbles, spiritual entities or whatever you feel most comfortable with.

- Close your chakras, open your eyes and carry on with your day.

Exercise 3.4 Learn to cut off energy vampires:

- Over the course of your day, make a mental note of everyone you interact with and how this interaction makes you feel immediately afterwards.

- Make a note of when you instinctively don't want to talk to or meet with someone, and how you feel if you go ahead and do it.

- Write down who you have interacted with that day and which of those interactions left you with less energy.

- Check for cords from these people and once you find them, remove them as described above.

- Close your chakras before you interact with them again and make a commitment to remain so while you are in contact with them.

- Be aware and make a mental note of all attempts to open you up again – pity, charisma, promises of help, guilt, etc.

- Check how your energy feels after you interacted with them in an energy closed-off state.

- If you feel unable to maintain the closed-off state, cut the connection for a while.

3.5 How to repair your energy mistakes:

- Ground, cleanse and protect your energy.
- Visualise a person whose energy you have affected negatively.
- Visualise your energy in their field.
- Call it back. When it comes back, cleanse it, then dissolve it, destroy it or dispose of it responsibly.
- Keep on imagining yourself clearing any negative energy you might have sent to that person until you find nothing else left.
- Say in your mind, "I give back all that is yours and I take back all that is mine."
- Visualise yourself detangling from this other person.
- If there are cords to cut, do this as described in Chapter 2.
- Ground, cleanse and protect yourself once again at the end of this exercise.

4.

Know: When intuition speaks, listen

Sometimes we just know. We look someone in the eyes and we know if he's telling the truth or not. We answer the phone and we know whether it's good or bad news. We listen to a presentation and we have a nagging feeling that something is not quite right, and yet we can't put our finger on what it is. We meet someone and we know if we can fall in love with that person or not.

This *knowledge* is how your energy talks to you. Some people call it intuition. It is the sum of all the energetic clues you pick up about a person, a situation or a place. It is the sum of all the invisible reports that have been presented to you and subconsciously processed in you. You may know that you know or you may not yet detect that voice. You may trust it or not. Or you may mistake it, sometimes, for other voices that rise up in you. But whether you have made peace with this *knowledge* or not, it is still there, living deep inside you.

So, if all this is in us already, how can we know what we already know? Or rather, how can we consciously access all this knowledge that is readily available to us?

Know the state of your energy

Practising grounding, cleansing and protecting your energy will help you develop a clear sense of the state your energy is in. You will begin to automatically become aware of when you are ungrounded, when your energy needs a cleanse or when you need to top up your protection. The awareness you have developed on the possible leaks of energy will give you information about whether your energy is fine or not.

All this awareness forms a very important base for *knowing* your energy. If you pay attention to how it feels, you will instinctively know when it does not feel right. This knowledge comes from the practices you have established for grounding, cleansing and protection, and from doing them consistently. The optimum practice would be twice a day, in the morning and in the evening. The minimum practice would be once a week.

The knowledge you build then becomes the fundamental base of those practices calling your attention whenever you need to ground, protect and cleanse. The more you trust it, the more this *knowledge* becomes part of who you are.

Become familiar with the state of your energy. When it feels good, how do you know it's good? How do you visualise it? What images come to your mind when you clean your energy field? Know these images, keep them in your awareness.

Also know the typical symptoms you experience when your energy is being interfered with. If you get irritated often, learn to recognise this sign. It may mean you need an energy cleanse. If you have a sudden, unexplained pain in your ear and then later on find out that someone was saying negative things about you, learn to recognise that symptom for what it is. Of course you cannot stop someone talking badly about you behind your back. The point is not to do something about it. The point here is simply to know. Hold the knowledge. Honour that knowledge in you: it is there to increase your power.

Know what gives you energy and what takes away from it

In addition to knowing the state of your energy, pay attention to what increases your energy and what decreases it.

People, situations, places

Some will make you feel better, some worse, and some will have a neutral effect on you. Keep your awareness active. Even if you cannot avoid certain people or situations, simply hold the knowledge of what this interaction tends to do to your energy. Over time, it is this awareness in you that will show you innovative ways to avoid toxic people or environments, or how to vary your protection routine according to the type of people or situations you encounter. All you need to do for now is keep that knowledge alive.

Daily routines

Know how you feel on a day when you did your grounding, cleansing and protection routines and how you feel when you didn't do them. Experiment and pay attention to the results. Realise what works for you and what does not. There might be days when you have no time to do a full grounding, cleansing and protection ritual. It's not the end of the world. But pay attention to how you feel. Remember it.

Health

The energy available to you greatly depends on the state of your physical health. Know how much sleep you need to operate at peak performance, what you need to eat and drink, how much exercise you need to do. Know what works for your body and what does not and hold that knowledge even when you don't do those things. If you stay out late one evening, have a lot of alcohol and eat the type of foods you know are not good for you, just observe it. Don't punish yourself for it; don't think negatively of yourself. Give yourself permission to do the things that are not good for you once in a while. But hold that knowledge. The key is to hold that knowledge without self-judgement. Often we prefer to ignore this *knowledge* in us because we cannot hold it in an emotionally neutral state. If I allow myself to know this work environment is toxic for me, how can I come to work here every day? So I'd better push that *knowledge* away and pretend that I do not know. Well, there is another way to deal with this. I can allow myself to know that this work environment is toxic for me and still continue to come to work every morning doing the best I can to ground, cleanse and protect my energy but without having to punish myself or justify myself in any way. Accept this truth. It is this knowledge, kept alive in you, that will eventually offer you a solution, that will allow you to change the environment. This does not happen overnight but once you accept the truth consciously your power increases, and with that the capacity to manifest the life you want also increases.

Know that you don't consciously know sometimes

Sometimes you might not know. You don't know whether a situation is good or bad for you, you don't know which alternative is the best choice. You get conflicting messages from a person and you don't know whether to believe them or not. Allow yourself to not know. It's ok. Being aware that you don't know something is the first step towards finding it out. There's tremendous power in not knowing. Hold that space open and knowledge will come to you.

Knowledge comes from a place of stillness. You don't need to do anything about it. Not yet. Before you do anything, simply know. Be there, with the knowledge that arises in you. It may say you don't want to live in the country you are currently in. That's ok. Carry on living there for a while holding that knowledge. See what happens next. Knowledge does not need to be followed by action immediately. Knowledge needs time to exist, simply to be. Give it the time that it needs.

Where knowledge comes from

It comes from inside your physical or energy body. Even when it comes from the outside, it will have no effect on you until your mind, your body, your heart or your guts process it.

Your mind

Your mind talks all the time. Sometimes it helps you see clearly the pros and the cons of a situation. It helps you synthesise concepts and analyse ideas. Other times in projects, it fabricates reality, it talks to you about the things it fears or the things it likes to worry about. Your mind is also influenced by the cultural or family conditioning you have assimilated. It will repeat things your parents told you when you were little, whether they were true or not. It will hold subconscious patterns, unresolved situations. It will attempt to compensate for not knowing by fabricating scenarios. It may also run repetitive thoughts until they become a program, a script that runs in the background of which you may not even be aware. Learn to discern the voice of your mind but know that it does not hold the ultimate truth.

Your heart

For a long time it was thought that listening to your heart equalled listening to your emotions. Emotions come and go and can be guides just as poor as the mind when it comes to *knowing* the reality. When we are happy, everything tends to be great. When we are sad, everything is bad. But your heart chakra is not only the centre of your emotions: it is also the holder of your own supreme knowledge. If you want to learn what is the real core of a situation, focus on your heart chakra and ask the question from there. See what answer comes back. Compare this answer to the one delivered by your mind.

Your guts

The gut feeling has been praised in business environments as an antidote to too much thinking. It connects you to your instincts. It can tell you instantaneously good from bad, right from wrong. Flight or fight. However, it can also get mixed up in emotions, in the past, unresolved patterns or situations. It can easily be polluted by fear, guilt and insecurity. It can also be heavily influenced by other people's energy, since it is the location of the solar plexus chakra and sacral chakra and these are two favourite places for negative cords to develop. If you absorb other people's emotions or thoughts, these are likely to reside in the gut, clouding your judgement. The gut feeling is a precious indicator but it's not the only one to listen to.

Your body

Overall your body has valuable information for you. It will tell you when it feels comfortable with a certain situation and when it does not. If you go for an interview and your body automatically adopts defensive positions while you are talking to the people you are considering working with, listen to that feeling. It tells you no. If your body relaxes and feels pleasure when in certain places, with certain people, this is giving you information.

Knowing the voices of your body, your mind, your heart, your guts and the overall state of your energy helps you maintain and increase your power base. Again, just *knowing* is enough. Hold that thought, hold that awareness. You don't necessarily need to do anything about it, not just yet. Connect to the power of that awareness before you decide to take any action.

Turn to the end of the chapter and do exercise 4.1.

Power sources

Throughout our lives we accumulate tons of information about what works for us and what does not. We sometimes hold on to this knowledge, other times we let it slide away. But if we stop and think, we each know what we need to operate at our best.

Take some time and fill in the answers to these questions:

- What are the best foods for giving power to my body?
- How many hours of sleep do I need to function at my best?

- How much and what type of exercise do I need to do for my body to perform at its best?

- How often do I need a holiday?

- What type of holiday recharges me best? Mountains? Sea? City? Backpacking? Luxury resort? Sports? Adventures?

- Who are the people in my life that bring out the best in me?

- What type of work environment/corporate culture is best for me?

- What type of people do I need to work with to be performing at my best?

- When I feel my energy is low, where and how do I recharge in the best way?

Don't spend too much time thinking about it; just write down the first thing that comes to mind. Let the knowledge that already resides in you come to the surface. Know your blueprint for high energy.

Passion as a source of power

There's one power source that stands out higher and taller than the answer to any of the questions above. There's one shortcut your soul has given you to help you build and maintain your power, one thing you were born with and that no one can influence or take away from you: your passions.

Passions are greatly overlooked and their potential to heal us and bring us back into our power base has been largely ignored. Described as hobbies, they lose importance, lose weight; they become disposable. A hobby is what someone does to kill time if he's got time to kill. A passion, on the other hand, is what our soul longs to do, what we were born to do, and doing exactly that gives us amazing power.

Don't think of your passions as hobbies, don't despise them, don't put them last on your list. Make time for them, allow them space and weight in your life. Make peace with them. For whatever reason and from wherever they came to you, they are here for a purpose. They are your secret power-replenishing engines. Follow your passions and you will enjoy more personal power, joy and meaning in your life than you ever thought would be possible.

But in today's world, which discourages personal pursuits and idealises hard work, how do we find out what our real passions are? We have been educated to fit into a 'socially acceptable' frame. Go to work, raise a family, socialise with friends. Go to the gym. Take a holiday. Repeat. In this never-ending routine, we might feel sometimes that we actually have no passions, and even if we had them once, we lost touch with them long ago.

Your passions are with you for a lifetime. Rest assured they are still there. Once you look for them, they will start slowly coming out of hiding. Just don't call them hobbies. Recognise the enormous energy gift they hold for you and honour them. Start by calling them passions.

Turn to the end of the chapter and do exercise 4.2.

Passions are things we are drawn to doing, and while doing them we lose awareness of ourselves. Time stops. We are so focused, we are so concentrated on doing that activity that we exist only in the present moment. Passions come easily and naturally to us; we feel we instinctively know how to do this and have been doing this forever. They are often our natural talents. Or even if it's something totally new and difficult, we feel that no pain is too great to learn how to do this. Passions are always there; even if you do not do that activity for a long time you instinctively feel a sense of pleasure when you do it again. Passions are things you do for pleasure – not for money, recognition or because they are part of a plan. That is not to say that money, recognition or following a plan cannot tie in with a passion. They can, but they are not behind the drive for it. Passions cannot be faked; they are either there or they are not.

Cooking, dancing, playing an instrument, painting, collecting stamps, writing, sports: all these are forms of passions. Travelling, exploring new cultures and learning new languages can be passions too. Someone can learn a new language out of a feeling that they have to, that it's part of a plan, but this will feel quite different than when the learning comes out of a passion for that language, culture or country.

Passions often make themselves known in childhood and accompany us through our lives. Other times we stumble upon them unexpectedly and they stay with us forever. They are there for us when we remember them and they reward us with a sudden increase in energy every time.

I knew how it felt to ride a horse before I ever got on one. I have no idea where this came from. It's always been there with me, in me. I dreamt of having a pony but this was not an option during my childhood and it never happened. So I just contented myself with riding horses in my dreams.

Then, one day, I must have been about twelve or so, I passed a place where people were riding. I became so excited. I told my parents about it. It took some time but I convinced them to let me have a go. I mounted a horse for the first time in my life and it felt just like I always thought it would. For a couple of years afterwards, I went riding once a week and my whole world revolved around that hour. Then I got a pair of riding boots from my parents as my fourteenth birthday present. I thought it was the best gift I'd ever received.

Then other things got in the way and I stopped riding. My teenage years passed by in a blur. I might have tried again once or twice, no more. I still experienced the same pleasure while doing it but I had other things to do so it just got left behind.

In my twenties I must have ridden a couple of times and then once again in my early thirties. The riding boots remained hidden in the attic of my parents' house. I had a busy life, too busy for riding.

Then, one day in my late thirties, after a number of failed relationships and lots of heartache, I hired a love coach. I wanted someone to tell me how to do this dating thing right. She asked me what my passions were. I shrugged, irritated, and told her this was not the issue. She said it was. Reluctantly I agreed to give up talking about finding love and look back at what I could do to love myself.

"What did you enjoy doing as a kid?" she asked me. And then it came back to me, a huge force like an explosion that blinded me momentarily. When I could see again, my boots, out of hiding, were dancing in front of my eyes.

"Riding," I told her. And then I told her about my boots.

"Well why don't you do that again?" she suggested.

I went searching for my boots in my parents' attic, in a different country from the one I was living in at that time. I found them and brought them back home with me. They stayed there for a while, a strange presence in the living room of my London flat.

Then, one day about six months after I brought them back, I found out that a colleague at work had just had a polo lesson. I instantly decided to join her for the next one.

For the next six months, my twenty-five-year-old riding boots found their way to a polo arena as I trained and learned the game. They got ditched eventually when I bought proper polo boots for my first game later that year. I had become a polo player. And I played with passion.

Polo gave me access to a reservoir of huge physical and emotional power inside me that I had never tapped into before. It changed my life. It brought deep friendships and amazing experiences into my life. I wrote about it and published my stories in a blog (www.seven-and-a-half-minutes.com). I travelled to Argentina because of it and found a second home there. It eventually brought love into my life as well, but that's another story.

And all because of that lady who asked me what I loved to do when I was little...

Find your passions. It's the most important thing you can do for yourself. It's the highest expression of self-love. Rediscover them and honour them. Listen to their call and see where they lead you. You might be surprised. There is more about finding your way forward in the following chapter; for now, what's important is that you become aware of where these power reservoirs lie in your life.

Listen to what you are being told

The bulk of *knowledge* will always be inside you and by doing these exercises you will increase your awareness of your power sources and the information your mind, your head, your guts, your body and, overall, your energy is trying to give you. The more skilful you become at listening to your own self, the more you will receive the message from the outside.

This is because the universe is talking to us. Continuously. Whether we pay attention or not, whether we believe the message is for us or not. Every moment we are being told, shown and directed. We are being helped. Once we become aware of this and accept the knowledge that is given to us, our power base gets another big lift.

The types of people you meet, the situations you get yourself into, the accidents that happen to you, the message on a billboard you pass every morning on your way to work. Life talks to us. If you look at everything through these lenses, life suddenly takes on a new meaning.

The only thing we need to do is ask: what is the universe trying to tell me?

If every time I send my CV for this type of job I end up with this type of boss, what does that tell me?

If my car will not start in the morning every time I have a meeting with certain people at work, what is that trying to tell me?

If I see a billboard saying "Go for it" and the next second a person rings to offer me a new job, what does that tell me?

If I keep on meeting people who have the same story in common, what does that mean for me?

For a while before starting to write this book, I kept meeting people who were stressed and close to burnout, working in corporate environments. What was that trying to tell me? As soon as I started writing this book, I stopped meeting those people.

Pay attention and notice the coincidences, the synchronicities and the messages, even if you do not understand them. Giving them attention is the first step. Simply notice, and ask in your mind: what is this about?

Sometimes the meaning will be clear. If you're being told three times a day to slow down in various circumstances, maybe keep that in mind when you deliver a presentation later that afternoon. Maybe the message was for that specific occasion.

Whether you understand the message or not, it's important to listen. Stay alert; receive what you're being given. The more you are willing to receive and the more attention you pay, the more clarity you will eventually have.

Questions and answers

We are trained all through school to focus on answers. To think answers are more important than questions. We treat answers with a lot of respect and overlook the questions.

But questions hold power. The ability to ask the right questions increases your power even before you get the answers. To get to the answers, it is fundamental to first ask the questions. That means being open to not knowing. Hold the space empty for a while; let the answer come from there. If the space is already taken, you cannot get an answer.

You may want to change your job but are not sure where to go next and can't deal with uncertainty. So you decide to make a lateral move to a competitor. You have already filled the space where an answer could be formed. A different answer. If the place is filled, a new answer cannot appear. And you may lose the opportunity to find a better work environment.

Just practise asking the question and then pausing. Let the answers come to you. From the inside: from your body, your mind, your head or your guts. From the outside: from people who talk to you, ads you see on TV, a song that plays on the radio. Leave space for the answers to come to you. Be an observer, slow down so that you can get the message when it comes. Because it always does. And no, it's not just your imagination playing tricks. When you ask a question and pause long enough, it's very likely you will get an answer.

Turn to the end of the chapter and do exercise 4.3.

The flipside of listening to signs is that sometimes we fabricate them in our own mind. In a desperate need to be told what to do next, we think we see coincidences and signs where there are none and we force decisions because of these imagined signs.

Signs are easy to fabricate. A fortune teller tells us we will fall in love with a man whose name starts with A. We meet a man called Andrew and we think it's him. Not necessarily. We love spaghetti bolognese, we go on a date with a girl who loves spaghetti bolognese as well and we think "That's it! It's a sign that we are meant to be together." Not necessarily. You go to work in the morning and find your inbox jammed with emails about a certain business opportunity. Incidentally, you also read about the same opportunity in the newspaper when you had your morning coffee. It does not necessarily mean it's the right business opportunity for you. When the universe talks to us, it does not shout. It usually whispers. The messages have a sense of timelessness and easiness about them. For some reason they catch your attention and stir a feeling inside you, most of the time a feeling which initially has no name. It simply touches you.

Over time, if you ignore what you are being told, the messages tend to get louder and louder, but this happens because we don't want to see them or accept their meaning. For instance, exhaustion and sickness are forms of repeatedly ignored messages.

Signs we look for are usually not real signs; they are the territory of fabricated imagination. On the other hand, signs that come to us unexpectedly and which touch us even before we understand what they are about are probably real. For instance, let's say you are trying to decide whether to go to the seaside or to the mountains for your holidays. You have been thinking about this for a few days and still have no answer. You need to make a decision today. Just as you enter the coffee shop to buy your morning double skinny cappuccino, you hear a song that immediately brings tears to your eyes. You are not sure why but you notice this. Then you remember it's a song you often heard as a child at your grandparents' place. Those were happy times for you. And your grandparents lived by the sea. There's an answer to your question. You did not look for this sign, you did not plan to hear the song, and moreover, you were touched by the song even before you realised why or the connection to your question. This is very likely a true sign.

Similarly, if you ask a question and get an answer in your mind in the form of a picture, and you try to change that picture – say it's a green meadow, you try to make it blue in your mind and you can actually do it – it is usually the product of your imagination. However, if you see a green meadow in your mind and no matter how much you try to change it, it keeps on reverting back to a green meadow, it's likely a true sign, a true answer to your question.

Be aware of when you are chasing signs and stop doing this. The signs you find when chasing will be meaningless. Let yourself be surprised by those which come to you unexpectedly, welcome them and add them to your inner wisdom. They are an important part of it.

Turn to the end of the chapter and do exercise 4.4.

Listening to the signs does not equal listening to others. Other people will very rarely know what is really good for you and their advice will come loaded with their own personal agendas, experiences, fears and worries. If their energy vibrates at a lower level than yours, they will not be able to offer any meaningful advice for your situation. The best of friends will simply listen to you talk and encourage you to find your own solutions. Remember, listening to the universe does not mean asking other people what to do.

Listening is not feeling. It is not thinking either. Listening comes from a place of silence within us. Learning to listen gets us in touch with that voice deep within us that often helps us navigate our lives in the absence of clear markings: intuition.

How intuition works

Intuition is the sum of your *knowledge*. It is everything concentrated in one pot. The signs given to you by your body, the state of your energy, the feelings in your guts, the thoughts in your mind, the signs you receive from outside.

Intuition gives you shortcuts. You may be a highly trained management consultant with your laptop full of models, tools and analysis frameworks. You may walk into a company and take all these models out and conduct thousands of analyses and questionnaires. You may eventually find out what the issue really is.

Or you can sit down, have a coffee with the head of the department you are tasked with investigating and ask her to talk to you. About whatever she chooses. About how work is going, what her worries are, what keeps her awake at night. Where does she stumble? Just listen to her and if your intuition is developed enough and you are accustomed to recognising and trusting its voice, you will pick up the key issues from that one conversation. You can then do your analysis, use your frameworks and models and present them in a way that coincides with the rational approach dominant in our corporations. But the intuition would have saved you a lot of effort in getting there.

We each have different tolerance levels when it comes to intuition, and different levels of trust in its voice. Before we try to deepen our trust, however, it is important to hear it when it talks.

Intuition does not shout. It talks to you calmly. It does not get angry when you don't listen to its voice. It simply stays there, patiently waiting. Intuition is quiet, calm, balanced. When you have a burning desire to do something it can mean a lot of things, but it's likely not the voice of intuition. Intuition comes in clearly and quietly, says what is has to say and then gives you the free option to listen to it or not. Intuition can be ignored if you so choose, but inevitably you will remember the voice once you have made the wrong decision.

Intuition comes from your personal power and it's the sum of all the knowledge in you. Honour it and respect it. By doing so, you respect your own power.

Deeper guidance

There are critical times in life when we may feel we need deeper guidance. This, too, is available inside us. Spiritual or religious people will refer to this as praying, asking for guidance from your guides: those entities who are always with us, advising us with every step we take.

If you feel uncomfortable with this approach, you can refer to this as your higher self, that part of you which holds the wisdom, which knows, which can see the big picture. In difficult circumstances or when you feel so lost and so confused that you feel nothing else can help, ask the part of you which always *knows*. Trust that you have one and that you will find it. The following exercise will help you identify and communicate with your higher self.

Turn to the end of the chapter and do exercise 4.5.

If you feel comfortable with the concept of guides around you, spirits who are here to help and protect you, do the same exercise asking to talk to your guides. Depending on your beliefs, you can identify them as guardian angels, as power animals, as ancestors coming to guide you, or simply as the voice of truth inside you. See who comes forward, accept them and welcome them. Some of them might come in a completely different shape and form than you would have expected. Just accept them. Hold a meeting with them. Imagine them around a table, talking to you. Practise going back to your council every time you want to discuss an important decision or understand a deep issue. Talk to them as you would to trusted friends. And trust what comes back from them.

As you do this exercise, you might notice the knowledge that comes to you from your higher self or from your guides has a different voice than when parts of you are speaking. It will have a different voice than that of your mind, of your emotions or instinct. It will have the paradoxical quality of coming from the outside as well as from the inside at the same time. It will feel calm. Guides don't shout. Your inner self does not get angry. There are usually no accompanying emotions; maybe just a feeling of peace and recognition. At the same time, some of the insights you receive will touch you, profoundly and suddenly, and might even bring tears into your eyes. You will feel that what you just received is somehow inexplicably but deeply *true*. Trust that feeling. Trust the reaction that it produces in your body. If it's just your imagination, it won't have this power.

Go back to talk to your inner self or to your guides every time you feel the need to. Know they are always there for you and all it takes to be able to access their wisdom is a moment of silence, the faith that they will show up when you need them and help you find your way.

Finding your way

Finding your way is not an action, it is a state. It's the state of *knowledge*. You might have found your way even before you actually live it. Once it becomes clear in you, it already exists and it will appear in reality eventually. Similarly, a book exists before it is actually written. When the energy of the book gathers and becomes clear in the writer's mind, the book already exists. Its energy imprint has taken shape. It is then only a matter of time until it will manifest in the real world.

All things that come to be, first *are*. They exist in energy form. This is the main principle of manifestation. You can read more about this in the second part of the book. What we are concerned with here, however, is how to maintain a level of inner power, clarity and wisdom that allows this state of *knowledge* to rise and flow within us continuously.

This inner wisdom will help you shape the energy blueprint of who you are and what your life is all about. Once your energy is cleansed, grounded and protected, it will give you a sacred space where you can just be; where you can get to know yourself, your deepest desires and passions. You will become more receptive to what the universe is trying to tell you. Gradually you will trust your intuition more and you will build your own knowledge.

This process takes time. If you are starting from a place of energy depletion or if your own energy field has been loaded with negative vibrations, it will take time to build up your reservoirs to the level where you generate, gather and synthesise all the knowledge that is available to you. It will take time for your energy to increase to the level needed to support you in creating the life you want.

Just be patient and give it time. How long? Many years ago I came across one of the best descriptions of the concept of time I have encountered in my life. It came from West Africa. The people there say that it takes as long as it lasts and it will be over when it finishes. So, take your time; as long as it takes. Make a commitment to trusting the process and let go of the need for outcomes. Simply know that you are building your reservoir of personal power. Continue to ground, cleanse and protect your energy daily. Pay attention to your inner *knowledge* and build your trust in it.

Healing is a process that takes time. You heal a broken bone in six weeks. You wish it could be done faster but whatever you do, it will take six weeks. Similarly, emotional wounds take time to heal. If you rush them, you will only cover up their bleeding. Energy wounds also take time to recover. Give them the time they need. If you continue to build and trust your *knowledge* system, you will know when it has reached a comfortable level.

In addition to the regular routines of grounding, cleansing and protection, the most important thing you can do to heal your energy and give it time to replenish is to take time off. It's like an energy detox for your system.

Taking time off

Taking time off means exactly that. Take time off from your day-to-day life. Take a sabbatical from work. Tell your spouse you need some time off to resettle yourself. Go to a different place from the one in which you live. Take time off from your social life, from your daily obligations, from your plans and schedules. Just take time off.

The Aboriginal population of Australia has an interesting concept similar to time off. It's called *walkabout*. It's actually a rite of passage in which an Aboriginal male goes off by himself to spend six months or longer in the wilderness to make the transition into adulthood. Basically the purpose of the journey is to get in touch with their inner power and come back to the tribe as grown men ready to assume adult obligations. The modern rite of taking a gap year to go travel serves exactly the same purpose. In order to find out who we are we need to go look for ourselves, and this cannot be done in our usual day-to-day environment.

As adults, we may feel we don't need a rite of passage into adulthood any more. But we may need periods of time when all that we do is get back in touch with our own power. And the best way to do this is give it the time and the space to renew itself.

Our working lives are designed to revolve around short holiday periods: a few days off for Christmas, perhaps a week's skiing, or two weeks on a beach if we're lucky. Usually during the first days of the holiday, we are still wired into the habitual day-to-day rush of our lives. We check emails on the beach, we wake up early, and we still aren't disconnected from the problems we left back home. Towards the end of the second week of holiday, we start stepping into another world where the life we left back home starts to fade and we get in touch with different parts of ourselves; parts we have not felt for a long time. We might remember some deep, buried passion. We might get ideas about what we want to do with our lives next; we connect deeper to our families and friends, to nature.

Something strange happens if the break lasts longer than two weeks. By the end of the third week the feeling of dread about going back to the rush starts to dissipate. After four weeks it goes away completely, as if there's nothing to go back to; as if the life you had before happened on another planet. You start living in the present.

Assuming you have planned your time off well, you have taken care of your financial, social and practical obligations back home and don't have to deal with these worries, taking time off, longer than a usual vacation, is one of the most powerful detox boosts you can give to your energy. You give it time to heal, to resettle, to rest, to grow.

Taking time off takes you back to a white piece of paper, to time 0, to the point of creation. By taking time off, you send a powerful message to your energy. You say, "I am looking after you, I'm giving you an opportunity to grow and replenish yourself. Then you can tell me what I am to do next." Taking time off makes space for the new to come into your life. It is during this time of not doing that you actually build your strong foundations for your next phase of *doing*. We will discuss more about decisions and actions in the second part of this book, but for now what is important to keep in mind is that when you let a state of *knowledge* form in you, it will fit itself into decisions and actions effortlessly. You simply need to allow the conditions for that *knowledge* to develop in you, and paradoxically for this to happen you need to open yourself up to not *knowing* for a while.

A lot of people instinctively feel that they would benefit from taking time off, but they always find a reason why they can't:

How will I be able to get back into my life?

This is the myth of 'jumping off the train'. The train is our day-to-day life, usually going at high speed just like the lives of everyone around us. The strong, irrational fear here is, "If I jump off this train that moves on so fast, will I be able to jump back on? Or will I stay out there forever, watching the train go by and never actually being able to catch it again?"

Know that this is an illusion. By all means, plan your time off well, make sure you can finance it and make sure you put in place some safety nets to help you return to your life. But know that you can jump back on that train again. If you still doubt this, speak to people who have done it and then managed to get back on the train.

What if this hurts my career?

"How will I be able to explain this? Will anyone give me a job after I tell them I have taken six months off to go fishing in Alaska?" This is a conditioned fear. It comes from our education system, our collective paradigms, the myths we are conditioned to believe. When you talk to potential employers at the end of a sabbatical, just highlight all that this experience has given you, all the extra skills you will be able to bring to their workplace as a result of it. Maybe it's teamwork, or self-confidence, or the ability to deal with the unknown; perhaps a foreign language you now master. Remember your interviewer is a human being and at some point in her or his life, they too will have felt the need to take time off. If they have, they will understand where you are coming from. If they have not, they will feel inspired by your story. In very few cases they will envy you for it, and as a result will not give you the job. But you won't want to work for that type of person anyway.

What will I do afterwards?

This is the big question and it has to do with our tolerance of uncertainty. In our planned-out lives, this is a big break in the pattern. Remember this is exactly the point of taking time off: to let yourself not know what you will be doing afterwards. That you are willing to let the *knowledge* rise in you and are cultivating your own personal power, and that together they will tell you what to do next. And they will do so when the time is right.

How can I justify the money investment in doing nothing?

Our rational minds will always throw in the question of money. How much will this cost? How am I going to finance it? What do I have to give up to do this? By all means, consider these questions and think about options. Do the maths, know the numbers. Work out where the money might come from. Maybe you need to sell your car; maybe you need to work overtime for six months before you are able to do it. Find out the costs and plan how you are going to cover them.

And once you have done this, accept that there is no formula on return on investment that can be applied to this particular investment. But know that it's the best investment you can make. It's not a car, not a flat, not a new pair of shoes. You are investing in increasing your own personal power. And the car, the flat and the new shoes are all going to come from that.

What will the others say?

Well, they might support you or they might try to stop you. Remember people talk from their own agendas, their own worries and fears. What is right for you will not necessarily be right for them. Listen to what they say but at the same time don't allow it to divert your own inner knowledge of what is right for you. It may help if you use the white bubble of light protection technique as you talk to other people about your decision to take time off.

What will I actually do with six months off?

We are so used to doing what others want us to do that simply having the option of doing what we want might throw us off balance. What do I actually want to do with this time off? You may want to start by doing the exercise below:

Turn to the end of the chapter and do exercise 4.6.

Taking time off might show you a different side of yourself. You may find out that who you are is actually not who you thought you were. Or that you no longer are that person. Often we are not attuned to the changes in us simply because we don't give ourselves enough time to get accustomed to them.

At the end of a sabbatical there might be parts of you that you decide to let go of. You may decide to change your job or move to a different country. Or you may find that you are actually in touch with your power base, that you belong exactly to the job or the place you live in, and you are looking forward to returning to them. Whatever way you decide to go afterwards, you will do it with your energy renewed and your personal power base increased.

One way or the other, taking time off will be the biggest gift you can give to yourself. Take time off to smell the wind and see how it changes; take time off to build your *knowledge*, to come back into your power. Take time off simply to give yourself pleasure. Take time off when you need it and for as long as you need it.

I am looking at her and I can read the strain in her eyes. The same strain I detect in her voice. I know very well what she is talking about. I have worked for that company; I know how hectic things can be. I know how easily you can get caught up in the 'do more' trap, how much you can push yourself... how much you feel like you need to prove yourself.

And I know how extraordinarily tiring and depleting this can be. She knows it too, but she feels there is nothing she can do about it.

"How about taking some time off?" I ask her.

As I say the words, I almost feel how irritating they must sound. I have been in her position. I can imagine how irritating would have sounded if someone had told me that, years ago when I was feeling equally depleted, tired and hopeless. When I felt I had no choice but to carry on with what I was doing at the time, even if that meant feeling even more tired, depleted and hopeless.

She shakes her head and does not answer. Silence falls between us and the leftovers of the dinner we have just shared in this fancy restaurant all of a sudden become the focus of our attention. Where is that waitress? We could do with a clean table.

I look at my friend. I want to help her. I am listening to her telling me how she feels. I am trying not to give advice, to simply listen. But the question comes out of my mouth before I could catch it. "How about taking some time off?"

The silence is still there; heavy, uninterrupted. In the meantime, the waitress has come and cleared our table. No, we don't want any dessert. And no, I don't want to push her any more than I already have.

We start talking about something else. But then she comes back to the work story. She tells me she met up with an ex-colleague who took some time off after he was made redundant. He was a high-flying executive and it just so happened that he was not needed any more. So he was let go. Everyone secretly pitied him when he left. Then he came back six months later after travelling through South America. He came back tanned, fluent in Spanish and full of life. He told them he got a job over the phone while travelling. It just came to him via an acquaintance who called him up. He decided to take it and he was now back in the same office where he used to work but as a client. The job he took was with a client of his former company.

I listen to her story. I do not need to add anything; the story itself is helping me make my point.

"But what will I do if I take some time off?" she asks at the end, as if this is the most important question.

This is not something I can offer advice on. But I know that the most difficult part is done. Because when someone starts asking what she could do with six months off, it means she has already seen that she can actually do it.

How to develop your intuition

We all have intuition but if we have not practised listening to it, it can get a little rusty. The voice will still be there within us but we will need to rebuild the bridges we have left unused. The following are suggestions on how to start using your intuitive powers and how to build on them. Remember, energy follows thought. As we focus more on our intuition, it will speak to us more and more clearly.

Sense people and situations before you experience them

Practise tuning in to someone's energy or to the energy of a situation and read what this is all about. Practise reading the energy of people, tuning in to what they don't tell you and what is important for you to know. Practise reading the energy of a work situation. Does this deal want to be closed? Where is the obstacle? Trust the *knowledge* that comes out of this exercise.

Test your impulses

Once you have an impulse to do or not to do something, notice it. Remember to go back and revisit what this message was, once the situation unfolds. Did you feel like you should have been doing something which you did not do, and later found out it would have been better for you if you had listened to that voice? Or the opposite? This exercise will help you understand when it's the voice of intuition you are hearing and when it is other voices.

The water exercise

Pour water into the sink or a bowl. Dip your hand into it and play with it. Keep your mind empty. Draw circles, shapes or lines. Focus on it while remaining relaxed. As you do this let the *knowledge* rise in you. See what images or thoughts you receive.

The piece of paper exercise

Think of a situation. Then take a piece of paper and crumple it in your hand. Straighten it again then examine it for a while; examine the lines and the crumples, the designs it comes up with. Touch it and take it all in. As you do this, let your *knowledge* rise in you. See what images, what thoughts come to you about the situation you wish to resolve as you look at the crumpled piece of paper in your hand.

Pay attention to your dreams

Practise remembering your dreams. It can be handy to keep a pen and paper by your bed to write them down first thing after you wake up, before they vanish. Don't consciously try to make sense of them, just remember them. See what feelings they stir in you, where they point to. Give them a place in your consciousness and let the message they have for you become clear. Remember to ask the question and wait for the answer.

Write

Writing is an excellent tool for developing your intuition. Take a blank piece of paper, think of a situation, person, issue or whatever you want to work with, and start to write. Start with not knowing how you are going to continue and what you will be writing about. Just put down on paper all that you know about the person or situation on which you wish to focus. The more you write, the more *knowledge* will make itself available to you.

When you need a little help

Below you can find some suggestions for external aids in developing your intuition. As with the previous chapters, this is by no means an exhaustive list. There are a lot of resources available and a quick internet search will give many more options. Just pick and use what you feel is right for you.

Crystals

Amethyst assists with developing your intuition and psychic abilities. It also works well as a psychic protection tool. Emerald also enhances psychic abilities and since it is connected to the heart chakra, it helps you access knowledge that comes from the heart. Clear quartz will increase your overall intuition and offer powerful protection as well. It is also the master healer. Other crystals you can use to connect to your inner wisdom or guides are labradorite, black obsidian, black moonstone and lapis lazuli.

Meditation

Any meditation technique focused on the brow chakra will assist with developing our intuitive skills. The brow chakra, also known as the third eye chakra, is the centre of our intuitive abilities. Cleanse and protect this chakra regularly. When you open up your chakras, focus on opening up the flow in this chakra and visualise a beautiful, intense indigo beam emerging from your third eye and the corresponding area on the back of your head. Spend time visualising this flow, and cleansing and protecting it as well. Make sure you close down properly at the end of your meditation.

Aromatherapy

There are numerous essential oils that can assist you in opening up your brow chakra and strengthening your intuition. Camomile, sandalwood, jasmine, lemon and vanilla are some of them.

Food

To strengthen the brow chakra, consume foods that are indigo in colour. Aubergines, dark grapes and all berries that are dark blue or indigo can help.

Summary: How to build your knowledge

- Practise becoming aware of the state of your energy; what increases it and what decreases it.
- Allow yourself to be comfortable with not knowing.
- Be aware of the different voices in you and know what is talking: your mind, your heart, your guts, your body.
- Know your power sources and connect to them to replenish your energy.
- Rediscover your passions and use them as your fuel.
- Listen to what the universe is telling you.
- Practise connecting to your higher self or to your guides when you need deeper guidance.
- Take time off when you need it.
- Consciously take time to exercise and develop your intuition.

Knowledge-building Exercises:

> ### 4.1 Practise learning to differentiate between the voices that contribute to your sense of knowing:

- Sit comfortably, ground, cleanse protect and open your chakras.
- Think of a particular situation, person, issue.
- As yourself these questions:
    - ⇨ What does my mind tell me? Focus your attention on your head.
    - ⇨ What does my heart tell me? Focus your attention on your heart.
    - ⇨ What do my guts tell me? Focus your attention on your belly.
    - ⇨ What does my body tell me overall? Feel your entire body.
- Listen to what comes back and notice the difference in answers.
- Be prepared for some emotions to arise as you listen to these answers.
- Form the intention in your mind to remember what you have been told.
- Close your chakras and open your eyes. Carry on with your day.

> ### 4.2 Rediscover your passions:

- Sit comfortably, ground, cleanse, protect and open your chakras.
- Ask yourself these questions:
    - ⇨ What did I most enjoy doing when I was five years old? What gave me pleasure?
    - ⇨ How about when I was seven, thirteen, seventeen?

⇨ As a child, what did I want to do when I grew up? Record all the answers to this question and those that follow as they changed throughout the years.

⇨ What did I most enjoy doing at school? What subject fascinated me?

⇨ What always seemed easy to me?

⇨ When I am sad, distressed or angry, is there anything I can do that immediately brings me inner peace?

⇨ What have I always felt the impulse to do but have never done?

⇨ Is there anything I do that makes me lose track of time?

⇨ If I could do one thing for myself right now that would instantly increase my feeling of joy, what would that be?

- Write down the answers to these questions no matter how irrational they appear.

- Close your chakras and carry on with your day.

- Revisit the list after a few days and see if you can identify your passions.

4.3 Practise asking questions and holding the space open for answers:

- Sit comfortably, ground, cleanse, protect and open your chakras. Ask yourself these questions, either in your mind or out loud.

⇨ What do I need to do right now?

⇨ What does my body need right now?

⇨ What does my heart need right now?

⇨ What does my mind need right now?

⇨ Where do I want to be right now?

⇨ What am I being told right now?

- After each question, pause and focus your awareness on your senses, feel the clothes on your body, listen to the sounds you can hear around you, feel your breath moving in and out. Feel the empty space.

- If an answer, an image or a thought starts coming to you, let it come and don't force it, jump ahead or try to finish an unfinished sentence. Just observe what comes.

- As you observe the answers that come to you, hold an intention in your mind to remember them in your day-to-day life.

- Then close your chakras, check your grounding, open your eyes and carry on with your day.

4.4 Practise opening your awareness to how the world talks to you:

- When something touches you, stop and focus on it.

- Say in your mind, "I am receiving this message." Do so even if you don't fully understand it at that moment.

- Don't struggle; don't try too hard. Simply hold this intention.

- Go on with your day, and if the understanding of what the message was comes to you, welcome it. If it does not, don't worry about it.

4.5 Practise speaking to your higher self:

- Sit comfortably, ground, cleanse, protect and open your chakras.

- Picture yourself in a place of utmost tranquillity. It can be in nature: perhaps on the banks of a river, or on the beach, overlooking the sea. Somewhere where you feel happy, calm and relaxed.

- Keep this image in your mind until you feel you have fully arrived there.

- Then ask to speak to your higher self. Form this intention in your mind and hold it there as you relax in the landscape around you.

- Be patient for a while.

- When your higher self arrives, let them take the shape in which they want to show themselves to you, even if it seems odd to you. They might appear as different people or as an older version of you, as an animal, as a voice, or in a myriad of ways. Accept them as they appear and welcome them.

- Talk to them as you would to a friend. Tell them about your problems and your sorrows. Ask for guidance.

- Listen to what comes back. Some of the information might be surprising. Accept it.

- Talk to your higher self for as long as you feel the need to.

- Then thank them and let them go.

- Wait a while in silence. Let the knowledge you have received settle in you.

- Breathe deeply in and out. Keep breathing as you count to five in your mind, then open your eyes.

- Ground again, close your chakras and carry on with your day.

4.6 How to discover what to do with your time off:

- Sit comfortably, ground, cleanse, protect and open your chakras.

- In your mind, ask yourself these questions:

  ⇨ Where do I really want to be right now? Note what comes back to you: a place, an environment, a country, a landscape?

  ⇨ What is it that I always wanted to do and have been putting off?

  ⇨ Is there anything connected to my passions that I want to pursue right now?

⇨ What type of messages have I been receiving lately that can help me understand better what I want to do?

⇨ What would give me joy?

⇨ If I had all the money in the world right now and never had to work again, what would I do? Note: the question is not what you would buy with that money but how you would spend your time.

- Sit with your eyes closed and explore these questions, and any others that may come to mind.

- It may help if you have pen and paper handy to write down what comes to you.

- When you feel you have a good base to work from, take a deep breath, open your eyes, ground again and close your chakras.

- Put the list away for a day or so, then look at it again and see what you can pick up.

PART II
Rise High

5.

Decide: Use your intention to set the wheels in motion

Between stillness and action there is a point of maximum power. It's the point where we turn from the inside to the outside, from what we know to what we do. It's the fraction of a second when the first move is initiated and change is born. As with everything in the world of energy, this moment takes place in our energy first. It's the moment of the decision.

This moment has all the energy it takes to create the desired outcome. In the universe of your energy, the point of decision is the Big Bang, the point where creation starts. And yet before the Big Bang there was something else. There must have been an intention to have a Big Bang. That's why a Big Bang actually happened. Similarly, before a decision can be made there must be an intention. For instance, my intention is to have a healthy body. So I decide to join a gym. Or I decide to do something else that would support my intention. I would not join a gym if I had no intention pushing me to do so. But no matter how strong my intention to have a healthy body is, it will not materialise until I do something about it.

Before things exist in the real world, they exist in energy form. Before an illness hits your body, it will hit your energy field. Similarly, before you create something in your life, you create a base for it through an intention and set it free with a decision.

The power of intention

Intention is a thought, a desire. Something like, "I want to feel passionate about the work that I do." Or "I want to learn to play tennis." Or "I want to be able to speak Chinese." It can be anything you decide to bring into your life. This intention that you formulate in your mind, like all thoughts, has energy. When the intention is set consciously, this energy can hold amazing power. We ground, cleanse and protect our energetic field with the help of our intention. The changes in our energy are real even though they are set in motion only by our thoughts and imaginations.

A dancer waits in silence for the music to start but already has an intention to dance. When the sound comes, she lets her body flow effortlessly. Similarly, our decisions will spring from the state of stillness we have allowed to gather inside us and they will move us effortlessly into our life dance. And the moment of our decision-making is like the first note of the tune. It's the moment when stillness becomes action.

Similarly, an intention we hold as a thought in our minds can bring about real opportunities in our lives. But these opportunities will need to be taken and for this we need a decision. If there is a strong enough link between the intention we form and the *knowledge* we have accumulated, the opportunities we are offered to turn our intention into reality will arise naturally and we will feel comfortable making the required decisions. For instance, I have an intention to feel passionate about the job that I do. I have accumulated enough *knowledge* inside to tell me what type of work I enjoy doing and what I don't. I know I work well with people and like to travel. I also happen to have an intention to see the world. I also really love ancient history. I am aware that I would love to have a job that would allow me to travel and see the world rather than work on spreadsheets as an analyst in the marketing department. I have no idea how ancient history could be linked to all this but I keep the knowledge that this is something I would love to be connected to. I now start to talk about my intention with the people around me, I go on the internet and search for what type of jobs are out there that will allow me to travel the world and meet new people. Maybe I don't try to link anything to ancient history just yet. For a while nothing happens, but I keep on strengthening the link between my intention to feel passionate about my job and my knowledge of what it is I enjoy in a job. One day a friend tells me about an opportunity to work as a tour guide in Rome. Wow, this job could potentially have it all, I think. But it will be something totally different from what I do today and change is always scary. Will I be able to do it? Will I actually like it? Will I be all right moving to a different country? What if it's a mistake? I look at the phone number my friend has passed me and I wonder whether I should call and apply for an interview or not. This is the moment of my decision. The intention was there, the *knowledge* was there and the opportunity came. But it could all mean nothing without my decision to dial that number.

Intentions can be old or new. Some intentions have been with you all your life and yet never led to anything. Maybe you always wanted to speak Spanish but you never learned it. That's ok. Their time will come. On one condition though: that you hold that intention consciously in your mind. Other intentions may be more recent, they might just pop up in your mind. Whether old or new, accept them consciously, feel them; own them; hold them and then let them go.

Why let them go? Because for an intention to be able to manifest, we have to let it go out there in the world. We have to give up the attachment we feel to it. We have to detach ourselves from the outcomes. If we don't, if we obsess about it day and night, what we are doing is actually holding on to it and stopping it from going out into the world. Remember, energy follows thought. Release your intentions by not thinking about them all the time. Trust that your intention will manifest in reality without you constantly, obsessively thinking about it.

Turn to the end of the chapter and do exercise 5.1.

Your intention, released into the world, will set in motion powerful wheels that will bring opportunities for that intention to become reality. And when the opportunity presents itself, you still have one more step to take. You have to make a decision.

I had always wanted to go to Africa. One day, when I grew up. As a kid, I often got asked:

"What will you do when you grow up?"

"Go to Africa," I would answer.

I am not sure where this desire came from, or when it appeared, but what I remember clearly is that all throughout my childhood I dreamt often that one day, when I grew up, I would go to Africa.

Then I grew up, and I did not go to Africa. I went to university instead, got a degree, got a job, went on holidays, fell in love, moved in with a guy, broke up with the guy, moved to a different country, started another degree, got another job, fell in love with another guy. My life was busy and Africa had no place in it.

By my late twenties, I found myself trapped in a corporate life I did not want, working for a company I did not like and living in a country I felt I did not belong to. I did what I knew worked in the past: I started sending out CVs, thinking that another job, another country and another company might be right for me.

And then Africa came to fetch me. It came via a small ad on the Lonely Planet website, which I was browsing absent-mindedly one Monday morning before the start of my working day, just to let my mind wander and plan my next holiday.

In the travel forum, someone had posted a small announcement: "Got a Land Rover and planning to drive from London to Cape Town. Looking for two others to share the costs and the adventure. Leaving in three weeks. Application still open."

It was 'application still open' that caught my attention. As a joke, I sent the guy my CV, the same one I had sent to dozens of companies in the previous weeks.

Intention will bring you the opportunities but will not do the work for you. When the opportunities come, you have to take them. You have to make the decision, to say yes.

This moment of decision can be one of the most stressful and agonising of our lives. The pros, the cons, the mind, the heart: so many voices inside us and so much confusion. But it does not necessarily need to be that way.

Decision techniques

We each have our preferred methods for making decisions. We have chosen them because we feel they worked for us. Sometimes it is helpful, though, to be aware of other techniques and try them out, even if just to check they validate our decision. Decisions can be based in the mind, the emotions, the body or our internal, deeper wisdom which some people call our spirit. The really strong ones are a combination of all of the above.

Listen to your mind – the pros and cons list

The list of pros and cons is an established method for rational decision-making. Your mind is in control and loves the feeling. This method is quite simple. List your options. Then write down all the advantages and all the disadvantages of each option. Or call them pluses and minuses, or pros and cons. Write without thinking too much; list all that comes to your mind. Then read through all of it, all the pluses and all the minuses for each of the options, and see what emerges. The stronger alternative will usually stand out.

Listen to your emotions – the talking chair technique

This method taps into the emotions generated by each alternative you are considering. Pick a few chairs, assigning one for each alternative. Say this chair represents alternative A, this other chair B, etc. Distribute the chairs around a room. Then go sit in each chair and see how you feel. Tell yourself: "When I sit in chair A, I will feel as if I have chosen alternative A. When I move into chair B, I will feel as if I have chosen alternative B." And so on. Sit in each chair for five to ten minutes and try not to think of anything. Simply pay attention to how you feel. What feelings arise in you? If you find you have difficulty accessing your feelings and stopping your mind from talking, just focus on your senses. Feel your breath going in and out of your body. Listen to the sounds around you, feel the sensation of touch. Feel the part of your body that is in contact with that chair. Feel your feet on the floor. Feel you skin touching your clothes. Then feel whatever arises in you regarding the alternative assigned to the chair in which you are sitting.

Listen to your body – the ideomotor response

The body holds enormous knowledge about what is good and what is bad for us and can help us with decision making.

The ideomotor response is a technique initially used in hypnotherapy, which can help us with our day-to-day decisions. It is based on the involuntary, subconsciously produced movements of a body part in response to a thought, feeling or idea. There are several ways in which you can tap into this body knowledge and the easiest is the 'yes and no' exercise.

Focus on one of your hands. Tell your body to pick a finger to signal yes and another finger to signal no. Tell the body that the finger needs to twitch or lift according to the answer to a question. Then ask the hand to show a yes signal. Watch your hand and see which finger lifts. Don't try to do this consciously, simply watch your hand and wait for a finger to lift. Repeat the request for a yes response until you have a consistent response. Do the same for no. Ask a few times to see a yes response then a no response. Then start asking yourself questions and see which finger tends to lift. Do this without thinking too much about it; it's best if you can do this in a state of absent-mindedness, as if what is going on is not really important. Detach yourself from the outcome; simply maintain a sense of curiosity as you watch your own hand and notice which finger is lifting. Pay attention to the answers you get. Your body is talking to you.

Sometimes the movements can be very small: a simple twitch. It is still an answer. At other times, you may have trouble relaxing deeply enough to receive meaningful messages from your fingers. In this case I recommend you use your arms instead, as described below:

Stand up and lift both your arms, holding them at a 90-degree angle in front of you. Find your true or false signal. Ask yourself a question you know the answer to and then assign a yes/no correspondence to each of your arms. Then wait there with your arms outstretched without thinking of anything. Your arms will start to feel heavy and inevitably one will drop before the other. Just sense the heaviness in your arms and see which one tends to drop first. If the yes arm drops first and the correct answer to your question is yes, you have a truth signal. Then check your alternatives using your arms, assigning one per arm or asking yes or no questions and see which arm drops first.

Listen to your spirit – accessing our deepest wisdom

If you are a spiritual or religious person, you can think of this as getting help from the religious entities that you pray to or the spiritual concepts you believe in. If you are not comfortable with that approach, simply consider this as your higher self or inner wisdom talking to you. Whatever you want to call it, this innermost knowledge is available to us whenever needed.

The pendulum technique

A pendulum is any object that can be hung on a cord, usually a crystal. A pendulum works by indicating a yes or no answer as you hold it in your hand, your wrist relaxed but not trying to do any motions.

Pick a pendulum you are drawn to and ask it to show you a yes response, a no response and a maybe response. They might be a lateral movement, or a circular movement in a clockwise or anticlockwise direction. Check your yes, no and maybe responses a few times. Then ask your questions and see what it tells you. To people who believe in spiritual guides or helpful spirits, this will be a communication with these outside energies. To those who don't, it will be a manifestation of your innermost wisdom as it comes to the surface through involuntary and imperceptible movements of your wrist.

As you do this, be aware that your desire, whether conscious or unconscious, is a form of energy that can influence the outcome. If you are not sure that you managed to be totally detached from the outcome while checking, it is better to use this method in conjunction with several others.

Heart-based decision making

Your heart is your ultimate source of truth and wisdom. Heart-based decisions have been described for centuries as emotions overcoming thought, but this is not the true power of the heart. Emotions come and go and their very nature is this continuous change. But there is something much deeper that our heart can offer us: it can point out what feels true and what does not.

Heart-based decisions mean you ask yourself a question then close your eyes and focus on the location of your physical heart in your body. Bring your awareness there and imagine your heart. Stay focused there for a while and see what response emerges in you when you keep it there.

Practise this decision-making technique as you go on with your day.

As you do this, keep in mind that you are not looking for an emotional response. You are looking for a truth signal. The difference is that while an emotional response will feel strong, a truth signal will feel quiet, steady and solid. With time you will learn to make the distinction.

Praying for guidance

If you are religious or spiritual, simply ask for guidance when you pray. Then trust it will come and pay attention to the signs life shows you. If you are not comfortable with the concept of praying, hold the intention that your inner self will deliver the answer to your question. Similarly look for the signs around. A variation of this practice is to ask yourself a question just before going to sleep and make an intention to wake up knowing the answer. See what happens in the morning.

The power of imagination – what if you knew?

And then there is our imagination. We have been conditioned to consider imagination unreal and yet we hold on to illusions as if they are truth. Just as the illusions we consider to be true are not really true, imagination can sometimes be the way our spiritual self talks to us.

When you don't know the answer to a question, practise asking yourself this question: "And what if I knew? What would that look like? What would that be?" Then make it up. Allow yourself to make it up and play with it. Have fun. Again, you don't need to talk to anyone about this. Do it in the privacy of your own mind. Ask yourself: "If I did know what the best alternative was for me on this particular occasion, which one would I choose?" See what comes up and check this through some other decision-making techniques.

Turn to the end of the chapter and do exercise 5.2.

Power vs force

When we can't get in touch with our power, we turn to force. We start to force things rather than let them emerge naturally.

A healthy decision is *effortless*. Not powerless, but effortless. It has no force but it has power. We do not force it upon ourselves and we do not let anyone force it on us either. A healthy decision naturally emerges from the stillness in us, from the *knowledge* we have created, from our power base. A healthy decision feels easy, makes our body relax and usually flows towards implementation naturally. A healthy decision makes us feel joy, freedom, expansion and anticipation. Things in the outside world open up for us when we make a healthy decision. A healthy decision connects us to the world and makes us feel we are part of it. A healthy decision feels just like this: healthy. It will bring us energy.

A forced decision, on the other hand, will lack true power; it will be *powerless*. It will make your body cringe and close up. It will induce feelings of panic, of terror, of worry and dread. It will make you feel sad. It will make you want to justify your decision continuously, to yourself and to the others around you. It will constantly spark doubts and second thoughts. A forced decision is not necessarily a wrong decision in itself. It might be the right decision at the wrong time. Maybe it was too early for it. Maybe you were not ready for it yet. This in itself makes it a forced decision, and hence not a healthy one. A forced decision will need pushing and accommodating and will require large amounts of energy to take, maintain and implement. A forced decision depletes our energy.

When we force things to come our way, we don't enjoy them. We instinctively feel this is not what we are after. This happens because the amount of energy we spend during this process is far greater than the energy we get from the outcome. In the end it's not about what comes to us. It's about how it comes.

We force decisions sometimes because of the need to control reality. We feel we *should* do this or that and we talk ourselves into it. Or because we are not yet in touch with our power base and we don't trust it to show us the healthy decision. Or sometimes we force decisions because we get lost in illusions.

Truth vs illusion

Some things are simply true. Others are fabricated, created usually by our minds, but sometimes by the mind of others and from there poured into ours.

We hold illusions dear and we cling to them because they promise us a better version of reality. It's like a shortcut. Don't worry about doing the hard work, they say: just follow us. We will deliver you what you want and it will be ok.

Illusions arise in us to cover for the lack of awareness. When we are not in touch with a part of ourselves, or are not aware of it, we usually build an illusion as a quick patch-up. If I am bad at relationships and I find only the wrong guys to date, I build up the illusion that one day I will meet Mr Right. This illusion saves me from the hard work I have to do to confront my own relationship patterns. If I am not good at managing my energy and constantly allow energy vampires to feed off me, I am building an illusion in my mind that somewhere out there is the perfect job for me, with the perfect boss who, for a change, will not bully me. This illusion serves the purpose of helping me avoid looking at my own energy management patterns. We build illusions that life will give us what we want and we paint these illusions in bright colours and hang on to them with enough power to strangle an elephant. But guess what? When these illusions show their true colours, which inevitably they will because they are simply the fabrication of our minds with no support in reality, we get seriously blown off our feet. We become hurt, angry and desperate. We fight with the last of our strength not to let an illusion go. Why do we do this?

Because illusions hurt when they go. A part of us dies with them. That's the part that created them in the first place.

Truth, on the other hand, does not hurt. Truth always feels right, feels light. When something is true and we allow ourselves to feel that vibration, we recognise this feeling. It's got an 'it's ok' quality around it. This is valid even for truths that might feel emotionally painful at first. Once we recognise the truth in a situation we are able to accept it, even if it triggers a response of emotional pain at first. With acceptance, that pain dissipates. For instance, we may terminate a romantic relationship that was true, where love was real, and feel sad but light and ready to let it go at the same time. We may feel emotional pain when it ends but not the desperation, the clinging, the need to make it work at all costs. This does not happen when an illusory romantic relationship ends, where the love was not genuine. We fight and we plead and we hurt and we cling on then, because it's the very illusion we have created that we don't want to let go of.

Truth never dies. It simply transforms itself into another truth. What is true about you will always be there. What is true about a situation will carry on being true. Truth has no correspondence in time or place, it is a vibration that we all instinctively recognise in our hearts: it's the vibration of reality.

If a work situation is not good for you, there is truth in that. It does not necessarily tell you to go find another work situation. This might be a possible outcome but before you do this, get in touch with that vibration of truth and ask yourself "What is true about what I am experiencing right now?" When you find out the truth about a situation, you will get invaluable insight into what it brings to you. It will tell you why you are there, living that situation, what it was in you that attracted it, what you can change in yourself so that you do not attract it again, and what it had to teach you. Ask yourself what the truth is and let yourself feel its vibration in your heart.

Let's take a look at the most common illusions we create and cling to in our corporate lives.

I am not good enough. I have to prove myself constantly.

This is the main one. We inherit this from our school years and we take this with us into our working life. On a deep level somewhere inside us, we feel we are not enough and only constantly proving our worth keeps us safe. We strive for a good review, for the next promotion, for public recognition, in a desperate attempt to feel good about ourselves. See this for what it is: an illusion. No matter how much appreciation you receive from outside, it will never compensate for your own lack of it. Look inside, sort out your own self-worth issues and you will have a much more balanced life.

What if I fail? What if I lose it all?

This terror often accompanies us throughout our professional lives and it's linked to the "I am not good enough" illusion. Failure is seen as something bad, to be avoided at all costs. This is another illusion. Failure makes us strong and teaches us lessons; failing enough times means we have tried enough. A life with no failures is a life not fully lived and what you lose sometimes is worth losing. Recognise this fear for what it is: an illusion. And then go out there and fail a few times, just so you can get used to the fear of failing and get over it. Just like when you learn how to ski.

The company cares for me.

No, it does not. The 'company' does not exist in reality: it is just a concept. Some people who work there might care for you, others might not, some might wish you well, others might wish you ill. Some will actively try to sabotage you if it benefits them. Most of the people working in your company, though, will be neutral towards you and it won't matter at all to them what is happening to you. There is no such thing as the 'company'. Don't identify yourself with an illusion.

One day, I will do it.

The illusion of 'one day' in the future is a very powerful one. It helps us carry on not doing what we feel is good for us; it helps us buy time. The 'one day' usually never arrives and on some deeper level we know it will not, we know we are fooling ourselves at the very moment of saying it. Trust that *knowledge* and let it come to the surface. It will lead you out of the vicious circle of not doing what is right for you and postponing it to an imaginary 'one day' in the future that never arrives.

I have not got enough time to do this.

Time is what we make of it. Time in itself does not exist; it is a fabricated concept, a social convention and therefore an illusion. You simply can have the time that you chose to have. Playing polo has taught me that seven and a half minutes which is the duration of a period of the game also called a chukka is in fact an eternity. Lots of things can happen in seven and a half minutes. A lifetime of events can unfold. You can lose or win a game, have a fall and break your arms or stay healthy. You can score many amazing goals and have the game of your life. Seven and a half minutes is not really just seven and a half minutes. If you find your hours in the day quickly disappearing under countless appointments and things you have to do, question why you do this.

I need to work hard to succeed.

Says who? Your education? Your socially acceptable paradigm? Your group of friends? Your parents? Your boss? Who says that you need to work hard, to feel like you struggle every day and that this is how things should be? Just question this as you question the rest of the beliefs you were fed by your family, your education and your society. See if it's right for you. Maybe you need to work smart to succeed. Or maybe there is no such thing as success. Maybe doing what gives you pleasure already gives you a feeling of having succeeded. Maybe the concept of work itself is outdated and you can just think of it as finding what gives you joy and doing it. Simply question this belief and see what is left behind as you start to break it down piece by piece.

I have sacrificed so much for this, I cannot give it up now.

This is when your past decides your present. In economics this is called the concept of the sunk cost. A sunk cost is a cost you have already incurred. It's done. You have spent that money. It's in the past. Nothing you can ever do can bring you back that money. Accept this and let it go. Persisting in a bad investment means throwing good money after bad, losing more in the present because you have already lost in the past. Resist this illusion. Nothing you do in the present can turn your wrong decisions in the past into right ones. Simply judge a situation for what it brings you now. See if it's good for you or not in the present moment. Now.

I don't like what I do now but it will take me to a good position later.

This is when your future decides your present. The problem with the future is that it's unknown. It's hypothetical. It might happen, it might not. We may have a car accident tomorrow and die, and then there is no future. Or the person you are when that future finally arrives has no resemblance to the person you think you will be, looking ahead from this moment in time. I am not saying that we should live oblivious of the future. All I am saying is that we need to check if what we are doing with our lives right now makes sense for us or not. If the job you do today gives you a level of excitement, knowledge or passion you are happy with, do it. If you absolutely hate it and you simply do it because you believe it will give you something in the future, just know this for that it is: an illusion.

There are countless other illusions out there and each of us is a master in assembling our own toolkit. If you want to find out your favourite ones, here's an exercise for it.

Turn to the end of the chapter and do exercise 5.3.

Indicators of Truth

We might have a hard time dealing with our own illusions but the picture is not all black. In the middle of all this turmoil and hard work, there are some rays of light; some things that point true north and come to show us the way. We each have our system to recognise truth but there are some universal indicators that we can all relate to:

Stillness

Stillness comes from that place in you that *knows*. Through stillness you have access to your highest inner wisdom. If your decision rises from that place, like a wave that comes naturally from the bottom of the sea, it will have power and it will draw it from the still sea of *knowledge* you have built in yourself. When in doubt, just check and see what rises in you, and ask yourself if this comes from a place of stillness or from a place of turmoil. Feel your emotions, express them, talk to your mind, listen to it. Then let it all go and wait in stillness. And when stillness speaks, trust its voice.

Ease

Things that are good for us feel easy. Yes, this might go against the concept of hard work, but it's true. Decisions that are obviously good for us are easy to make. Activities that we're good at are easy to do. Concepts that we are genuinely interested in are easy to assimilate. Our passions feel easy to follow even if they actually require considerable investment in terms of time and effort. Trust the feeling of ease when it arises within you. Don't confuse this with the feeling of laziness. While laziness feels heavy and static, ease feels fluid and light. Trust it.

Joy

Joy is the deepest indicator of truth in our lives. Joy is the feeling we experience when we follow our passions. Joy is the feeling we experience when we deliver a piece of work we are very proud of. Joy is what points in the direction that is the best possible way for us. When a decision brings you instant and inexplicable joy, simply trust the feeling that it stirs inside you.

Flow

Good things that come to us simply happen. Often we have not tried hard to get them, we have not struggled for them. They effortlessly came to us. When you feel the flow in your life, trust it. See where it leads you. When a random phone call leads to an unexpected meeting which leads to a job offer, trust what this flow brings into your life. The best job does not necessarily need to come at the end of a long and painful application process. The best opportunities flow to us and this flow usually works in our best interests.

The moment of decision has enormous power. You can make things happen. All you need to do is accept the power you have and use it consciously. And then trust that the decision you made will move you ahead on your life journey and will help you unveil amazing adventures and give you wonderful experiences.

I did go to Africa in the end. I quit my job that day, gave up my career, my flat and my residence permit that allowed me to live in a country many people only dream of. I joined two total strangers in a car and spent eight months crossing Africa from north to south with them. I wrote a book about this trip (Through Dust and Dreams), a book that put me in touch with the joy of writing and started my career as a writer. I received countless emails from people who told me that reading my book had changed their lives, had helped them believe in the power of their own dreams. That book is still the achievement I am most proud of in my entire professional career. And I did get a corporate job again when I came back from my African trip, in a different country, for a different company, and it was a much better job than the one I had left behind.

Summary: How to decide

- ✔ Tap into the power of your intention. Form intentions consciously in your mind, then release them into the universe.
- ✔ Practise various decision-making techniques that take into consideration the input of your mind, your emotions, your spirit and your body.
- ✔ Learn to differentiate when you act from a place of power and when you are forcing.
- ✔ Recognise illusions for what they are.
- ✔ Learn to recognise the signals of truth in your life.
- ✔ Accept the power you have over your own life and the highest point when this power expresses itself: the moment of decision making.

Decision-making Exercises:

5.1 Set an intention and then release it:

- Sit comfortably, ground, cleanse, protect and open your chakras.

- Form an intention in your mind. This could be getting a promotion at work, a better job or an opportunity to finally clean out your garage. Anything.

- Visualise it as a ball of white light and release this into the universe.

- Bring your awareness back inside yourself and feel content just as you are right now.

- Remember that what you have done is enough for that intention to come true, and that you don't need to know the details just now.

- Then stop thinking about it.

- Open your eyes, close your chakras and carry on with your day.

5.2 Practise using various decision-making techniques:

- Sit comfortably, ground, cleanse and open your chakras.
- Think of a decision you want to make.
- Pick a few decision-making techniques and apply them:
  - ⇨ Use the pros and cons list to listen to your mind.
  - ⇨ Use the chair technique to listen to your emotions.
  - ⇨ Use an ideomotor technique to listen to your body.
  - ⇨ Use a pendulum or focus on your heart to listen to your spirit.
- Note where all these techniques are pointing: is there a consistent picture starting to form?

- Keep this knowledge in you and stay with it for a few days without actually making a decision. See how it evolves.

- Open your eyes, check you are grounded, close your chakras and carry on with your day.

5.3 Practise identifying and letting go of your illusions:

- Sit comfortably, ground, cleanse and open your chakras.

- Think of a decision you want to make.

- Identify all the thoughts that come to you regarding this decision and write them down.

- For each of them, ask yourself the question: "Is this true or is this an illusion?"

- Listen to the answers you get and how they make you feel.

- When you are sure you are dealing with an illusion, say in your mind: "This is an illusion." Don't fight it, don't try to prove it right or wrong. Simply hold this awareness in your mind.

- Form an intention to hold this awareness in your day-to-day life.

- Open your eyes, check that you are grounded, close your chakras and go on with your day-to-day life.

6.

Direct: Consciously choose to create the life you want

Life does not just happen to us. We make it happen. We are not some actor on a stage, playing a role someone else has scripted for us. We create our day-to-day reality and we do so every day, every hour and every minute. We do this through our actions, decisions, intentions, beliefs and most importantly we do this through the vibration of our energy.

Only when we accept full responsibility for our lives do we tap into our full power. Our life is ours to have, ours to change, ours to create. It is our dance with the universe. It is as good or as bad as we make it.

Directing our energy to create the life that we want has to do first with raising that energy to a level where it can actually create something. We achieve this by grounding, cleansing and protecting our energy. Then, it has to do with the creative power of our intention and the moment when stillness turns into action: our decisions. And lastly, it has to do with receiving what comes back to us and constantly channelling our energy in the direction we want to fly.

At this point, *doing* becomes less of a verb and more of a state. To effectively do we don't actually need to *do* that much.

When action rises effortlessly from your power base it will have a paradoxical quality: it will feel still. The struggle will turn into acceptance, chasing will become attracting, a sense of flow will replace the previous rush and you will glide forward smoothly and effortlessly.

Receiving vs doing

What we get in life does not depend on what we try to make happen. It depends on how much we can receive.

The supporters of the theory of scarcity will say that we all have to fight hard and struggle to get somewhere in life. That's because they see life as a constant competition for finite resources. The theory of abundance, on the other hand, says that there's more than enough for everyone and it is abundantly available to all of us. It only depends on how much we are prepared to receive.

We receive if we allow ourselves to do so; that is, if we question any limiting inherited or learned beliefs that tell us differently. We receive because we set the intention to do so. And most importantly, we receive through the state of our energy.

A person with a high energy vibration will be open to receiving more than a person with a low energy vibration. It sounds simplistic, but in order to achieve more we need to cultivate our ability to receive more. This is how you can do this:

- Keep your physical energy high. The foods we eat, the sleep patterns we follow, the exercise we do, the health of our body, the medication or drugs we take: all these will impact upon the quality of our physical energy.

- Keep your mental energy high. Think positively, declutter your mind, maintain an attitude of curiosity and excitement towards life, learn new things, keep a check on your mental chatter.

- Keep your emotional energy high. Do the things you love doing and do them often. Follow your passions, celebrate your successes, share your love.

- Keep your spiritual energy high. Meditate, feel your connection to the universe on a daily basis, be grateful, develop your spiritual practices and follow them.

- Practise grounding, cleansing and protecting your energy regularly.

- Ask for external help when you feel you need it.

- Surround yourself with people who nourish your energy.

- Frequent environments that increase your energy.

- Live your inner truth and express it often.

The more conscious we become of the quality of our energy vibration and the more we increase it, the more we are able to receive. And the more we are open to receiving, the more we will attract into our lives. This applies to all forms of energy: money, love, success, achievement, you name it.

As you focus on opening up to receiving, watch out also for these common limiting beliefs that tend to get in the way:

- Low self-esteem; feeling like we don't deserve good things.

- Self-doubt – "it doesn't work that way" type thoughts.

- An inherited or learned belief that life is difficult.

- Conscious or unconscious attachment to the 'hard work is good' concept.

- Loyalty towards your parents or family, especially if you come from a background involving struggle. This is a very strong one. If you love your parents very much and if they had to struggle all their life to make ends meet, it will feel like a huge subconscious betrayal if you can effortlessly achieve what you want in your life. Watch out for this, it is a common one.

- Fear of success that leads to self-sabotage. Ask yourself if you are actually afraid to succeed.

- Clinging on to illusions. Often we stop receiving because if we do, we will lose an illusion we have created and held on to.

- Clinging on to the past. In order to receive the new in your life, it is essential to let go of the old.

- The trap of 'not yet ready' when we feel we still have one more thing to learn, to finish off before we can actually enjoy the life that we want. This is a form of self-sabotage.

- Fear of losing connection. As you start receiving more in your life, you will lose those who are not yet able to do so. Your success and ease will become intolerable for someone who is not yet able to manifest these in their life. Accept this and let them go. Don't cling on to people, situations or patterns just because they were good for you in the past.

Flowing vs being stuck

Effortless manifestation has one clear indicator: it flows. Things come to us and they flow, one thing leading to another and then another. When this flow occurs in your life, don't be afraid to go with it. It will usually give you little visibility on the steps ahead. Those obsessed with control will distrust this flow because they cannot see all the coming steps. This is exactly the point. True flow does not come with any reassurance. It does not come with full visibility. Step two happens after you take step one. Step three does not even exist. It will be created as you take step one and become visible to you after you take step two. When you try to force seeing the things ahead, it will stop the flow.

If you get a phone call and someone offers you a new job that feels somehow unbelievably perfect for you, be open. I am not saying jump on it immediately but be open to exploring it. Stay with this feeling for a few days to see if it's authentic. See if it's real. Excitement comes and goes and illusion is often fuelled by momentary excitement. Joy, on the other hand, which is an indicator of truth, is stable. The joy you feel at the thought of a new job will be with you the moment you receive the call and the same joy will still be intact a few days later. Have the patience to check if the feeling is real.

If it is, flow with it. Agree to meet, explore, discuss. Visit their offices. Ask to be sent the job description in writing. Make it real. Take one step at a time and follow this flow. Don't skip stages. Don't just walk into your office and resign that very same afternoon. But do take steps: put one foot in front of the other and the path will be shown to you.

The state of flow comes to us but if we don't follow it, it drains away. The state of flow by itself cannot make things happen for us. It will show up when we have developed our energy to a high enough vibration that we start to resonate with it. But we will only follow it when we have developed our internal power to a deep enough level to trust it.

When we don't follow the flow, we get a sense of being stuck. This has very little to do with the circumstances of your external life. You may be doing the same job for ten years and still feel you are in a continuous flow. Or you may change job every six months and still feel you are stuck in a pattern of constant job-changing. Feeling stuck is not about what happens out there. It's a feeling you experience when the fear in you prevents you flowing. When you have said no to an opportunity that came to you simply because you were afraid of the unknown, this feeling of being stuck will shoot up and it will usually be accompanied by sadness. You will try to wash it away, to rationalise your decision, and if all fails you will try to cover it up with whatever you can: alcohol, drugs, too much work, keeping busy, going out. But the unease will still be with you, and it will tell you the winds of flow came to you and you said no to them.

In our hearts, we always know when this happens.

Attracting vs chasing

Once we are comfortable receiving and we have increased our energy level enough to hold all that is coming to us, we become conscious of the fundamental difference between attracting vs chasing. When you act from a place of inner stillness, you naturally attract more and chase less.

Chasing is what we do when we struggle. When we call ten times someone who does not answer our calls back. When we feel we are trying hard. Chasing comes from a place of worry, of fear, of low trust. We go chasing because we don't trust it will come to us. Chasing is fuelled by our insecurities, by our low self-esteem and by our own self-doubt. Chasing leaves us depleted, tired and somewhat sad. We often ask ourselves 'Why does life need to be so difficult?'

Attraction, on the other hand, is a state of receiving. We attract things to us because we trust they will come and we open up to them when they do. We attract by the power of our energy, by the high vibration we give out; we attract because we believe we will.

In Chapter 5 we explored the power of our intentions and how they fuel our decisions. When an intention arises from the *knowledge* we have built within ourselves, it will lead us effortlessly to a decision. I know what type of work I enjoy, I have an intention to find it, and I make the decision to go for it when the opportunity arises. This is all good, but what do I do in the meanwhile as I wait for this perfect opportunity to show itself? Well, I keep on directing my energy towards attracting this perfect work to me. I keep on energising my dream. How do I do this? I use the power of visualisation, and the next exercise will explain how you can do that.

Turn to the end of the chapter and do exercise 6.1.

The *Oxford English Dictionary* defines manifestation as an event, action, or object that clearly shows or embodies something abstract or theoretical. In other words an intention, which is something abstract, takes shape and form and becomes an event, action or object. It becomes real. Manifesting your intentions means exactly this: making them real.

Principles of manifestation

Before things happen, they have already happened in energy form. Before something is visible in our lives, we have already attracted it – we attracted it a long time before it came. We did so through the power of our intentions and the state of our energy.

As we become more comfortable with the concept of effortless manifestation in our lives, it is important to keep in mind some key principles on how to make this happen.

Keep it effortless

Whenever you feel like you are starting to struggle, stop. Take a deep breath; take a look at what you are doing and how you are doing it. Don't look at what others do or don't do, look at what you are doing. Sometimes it is easier to think that we struggle because *others* make us struggle. Turn your attention to what *you* are doing. This is often enough to stop the impulse to struggle. One of the best definitions I heard for this principle is "When you struggle, it means you are not doing it right." Stop and look at how you can do it better. When it starts feeling effortless, you're on the right track again.

Keep it clear

Be clear about what you want and you will get it. Sharpen your intention. Be specific about what you want but be open as to how this is presented to you. Being clear is about having a clear picture of how you will feel when it happens and what it will bring into your life.

Keep it open

At the same time, keep it open. You don't need to worry about how this is going to happen, what step twenty-five will look like and how long it will take. Simply send your intentions out there and keep yourself open. If you always thought your perfect job was in Italy, be open to a different alternative. Maybe it comes from Spain instead. If you always thought your perfect match would have blue eyes, be open to considering brown eyes as well. Maintain clarity about what you want to attract in your life but be open as to how you get to that overall feeling.

Keep it alive

Feel it, see it, imagine it. Want it. Feel the joy of it. Want it but do not become obsessed by it. That is because obsession creates blocks and pushes the object of your desire even further away. Let yourself feel how much you want it but without clinging on to it. Just give yourself permission to feel the joy this will bring into your life.

Keep it honest

When you try to follow other people's scripts for what you should have in your life, it will simply not work. What you attract will be based on their energy and filled with their conscious or unconscious desires. Not yours. Keep your desires personal. Originate them from within yourself and be honest about what you truly want.

Keep it playful

Don't take yourself too seriously. Just imagine this is a game and you are playing. Take the pressure off. If it does not come to you, it's still ok. Worry will lower your vibration and your attraction capability. Stay away from pushing, forcing or any form of desperation. Stay away from trying too hard, from treating it like a matter of life and death. Keep it light, keep it tranquil, keep it playful. Remember that even the Dalai Lama likes to tell jokes.

Let it go

Play with it for a while then let it go. Just release it to the universe. If you cling to it, it will not be able to leave, and if it does not leave it cannot come back as real. It will forever stay in the dream state. This is another paradox: what we most desire will only come to us once we let it go. Trust this as you do so.

So what are we doing when it all comes true? Let's say we have manifested the perfect job opportunity, the perfect romantic relationship; we have manifested the ability to earn enough to support the lifestyle we want. We are amazed at how easily this has all come to us and we are still a little bit afraid it may just disappear as easily as it came. Now what? What do we do next?

We live it. We accept it; we take it for what it is. We remember not to cling on to it. We continue to raise our energy and live our truth. We continue to attract; we continue to flow. There is no end to it. We make a commitment to ourselves to flow where life takes us. And to do this there is one other big commitment we are required to make: to live in the present.

Living in the present

When we live in the moment, we live in the flow. Flow does not happen if we are not living in the present. Flow cannot happen in the past. The past is stuck, it has already happened, it has a form and a shape, it is fixed, it does not flow. It can also not happen in the future. The future does not exist yet so it cannot flow. The flow can only happen in the present, in the moment that brings you one thing at a time, one step at a time, one decision at a time and one outcome at a time.

Live each moment, each thing and each step as they come, enjoy them, express whatever is trying to come up through you, honour the things that come to you, take them, live them. And then let them go if they want to go. Only when you do so will other things come. It's part of the flow.

When you are in a state of living your dreams, it will feel disappointing initially. This is because bringing a dream into reality makes that dream lose its alluring but unachievable shine. Making it real means covering it with a bit of dust. It's ok. Let the idealised dream go. And enjoy the dusty version of it. It's the real one.

What's the purpose of it all, you may wonder. Why do I have dreams? Why do I even try to achieve them? Why do I try to achieve anything?

Because things are waiting to come into this world and they can only do so through us. New concepts, new interpretations, new discoveries, new understandings, an increase of consciousness. A new book, a new baby, a new company. A new piano concert. A dance that touches the hearts of many who watch it and possesses enough beauty to help those people get in touch with the beauty they hold locked in their own hearts.

Whatever is trying to come up through you in this life, trust it and let it out. Once you find your way and live your flow, you will not fight it any longer, you will simply express it. And then let it go. Move on so that you can express the next thing that tries to come up through you. Don't get stuck. Remember to flow.

A manager will do this through the projects he will manage; an entrepreneur through the companies he will build. An executive who is in the flow and who works for a big company has the potential to touch the lives of many. If he or she comes from a place of personal power and inner peace, they will have a positive impact. On the other hand, an executive in a position of power in a company who does not have a grip on his own personal power will bring low vibration and low energy into the world. His deeds will impact negatively upon his environment and the people around him.

In the end it is as simple as this. Find your power. Live it. Flow with it. And then let everything else that wants to flow through you come into this world.

I have always known that working a nine-to-five job locked in an office was not for me. I have done it for years and all these years I knew it was not for me. I have taken breaks from it and then come back to it. I have found jobs that required me to travel a lot and those proved to be a little bit more bearable, since they were taking me out of the dreaded office. This helped, for a while. But inevitably they brought me back to an office and to the same nine-to-five routine.

As I started working on my energy, the flexibility of the jobs I attracted started to increase. I worked four-day-a-week projects that paid as much as my previous five-day-a-week ones. I had projects where it was perfectly acceptable to work from home for a couple of days every week if I felt like it and I did not need to ask for anyone's permission to do so. These were a lot better. I was feeling the pressure of the nine to five slowly but steadily decreasing.

And then, one day, it just went away. I was delivering another project for another top company, managing a cross-functional international initiative where most of the people I interacted with were based in a different country, in another time zone. I was still going to an office occasionally, although it started becoming more and more obvious that the only way I could deliver that project was if I was flexible enough to work late in the evenings to suit the time zone of my co-workers. I could do this, but not from the office.

I did not expect it to come so swiftly, so decisively and so clearly. But it did.

"I don't care where you are," my top client told me in the middle of a conference call in front of everyone who needed to hear it. "I really don't care where you are. As long as the job gets done, you can be anywhere. Work from home or from anywhere you like."

"From home – you mean from any home? Can I be anywhere in Europe?" I asked, still not believing how easily it had come to me.

"From anywhere in the world," he said.

I had not struggled to get this. I had not pushed, not forced it through. I had not spent countless hours awake at night thinking about how to make this happen. It simply came to me and I took it. I said thank you. And I asked for it to be added as a clause in our contract.

For the remainder of that project, I left London and worked from Spain. I moved there on an impulse, without a clear motive, just because I felt like it. I rented a flat in Mallorca and continued to do my conference calls, my emails and everything I had to do for the project. The work went well. And while I was there, I realised there was another reason I was there. I met a writer. We became friends and started touring the island together. She reminded me of my own passion for writing.

And then, after a few more dips in the sea and cups of coffee on my sunny terrace, the next step came to me. I was here to write a book, a book that was bubbling in me, asking to come out, and whose voice I had been ignoring for a while. I put one word after the other and started writing the first chapter.

This book was born here, in Mallorca. The title came to me while swimming. And then the chapters poured out one by one, in between conference calls and work emails. This book came to me helped by the constant feedback and encouragement of my new friend, the writer. And when the business project came to an end so did the book, because that project and this book had been mysteriously but strongly interconnected: one made the other possible and the other made the first one meaningful. They came together and then they both went away together, making space for something new.

And while working on both of them, I learned that when life comes to you, you live it, and when it pours out of you, you express it.

Principles of directing energy in the corporate world

At work we tend to place more importance on *doing*. After all, we are paid to *do* and very rarely to simply *be*. And yet, the same principles of manifestation that work in our everyday life will also work in our corporate life. In addition, some principles that are true in business can also prove true to our day-to-day life:

Optimum returns to scale, or when 'more is more' becomes 'more is less'

There is nothing wrong with the 'more is more' concept. Up to a certain point. If you pass a certain point, you suddenly find that more becomes less.

The Returns to Scale is a concept in economics that explains what happens to the output if you gradually increase the input. There are three laws governing this principle and a fourth, extreme one:

1. **Increasing Returns to Scale.** As input increases, output increases by more than the proportional change in inputs. In other words, the more we do, the more we get. The more we study, the more we know. The more we prepare for a presentation, the better we are able to deliver it. The more data we have, the better the decision we are taking. Up to a certain point, more is more.

2. **Constant Returns to Scale.** In manufacturing this is referred to as output increasing at the same rate as input. Looking at the bigger picture, you can think of it as 'more is equal'. After a certain point is passed, more data gathered or analysed for a decision will not increase the quality of that decision. Studying more for an exam will not influence the general outcome any longer. Checking the accuracy of a spreadsheet one more time will not have an impact on the overall accuracy any longer. Why is this? Because we have reached the 'enough' point.

3. **Decreasing Returns to Scale.** In manufacturing this is described as outputs increasing at a reduced rate from the proportional increase in input. Looking at the bigger picture, it means more is less. A time comes when the more you do, the less you get. Studying more for an exam the night before might make you feel too tired to actually be in the best shape when you take it. Gathering more data than necessary for an analysis might cause confusion and you might miss the main point. Over-preparing for a presentation might lead you to project a non-authentic and less credible image. We have all been there and we can relate to when more leads to less. Going further in this direction might push us into a fourth, extreme case:

4. **Negative Returns to Scale.** This happens when increasing inputs over a certain limit leads to a failure of the output. Looking at the bigger picture, this is when we have pushed ourselves so much that we need to take time off to recover. Or when we try to impress our new boss and show her so many things that we end up irritating her, producing the exact opposite effect.

Know where you are on this curve. Keep in mind that there is a point where 'more is more' turns into 'more is less' and if you keep pushing past that, you might end up with 'more is nothing'. Don't try to do too much. Find your point of optimum balance on this normal distribution curve and stick to it in everything that you do.

BATNA, or why a battle is won before it takes place

BATNA stands for the Best Alternative To a Negotiated Agreement and is a key concept in the theory of negotiation. It states that in order to have a strong point when you negotiate something, you have to have a strong alternative in case the deal fails. The stronger the alternative you have, the stronger your negotiating position will be and the more you will get from a deal.

So instead of focusing on the deal at hand, on getting the promotion, the job or the opportunity, focus on your alternatives. What happens if you don't get it? What's your best option? Work on strengthening this. If you want to ask for a pay rise, don't waste your time preparing all the reasons why you deserve it and how much it means to you. This is important, but not as important as your BATNA. Focus instead on knowing your market value, talking to head-hunters, having a few options lined up regarding what you will do if you don't get that pay rise. Feel strongly about your alternatives; feel happy about them. Then use this BATNA on the negotiation table. If your BATNA is strong there is nothing else you need to do. Your BATNA will win the battle for you.

Think about the "What if this does not happen?" question and work to strengthen and be happy with your alternatives. It will increase your power enormously.

This concept does not apply to negotiations only. It's a universal principle for life. In order for something to come to you naturally, you must be happy with how your life will be if it does not come. Construct your BATNA and be happy with it.

The change curve, or why we need to go down before we go up

The change curve describes the stages of transition in personal and organisational change, whether this change has been initiated by us or by others. It looks like a curve that first goes down then starts to slowly climb up again.

It goes down first because any disruption to the status quo will have an initial negative effect. No matter how prepared we are for it, how much we want the change to happen, performance will go down as we need to get used to the new. If change is not welcomed, this phase will be filled with shock, denial, anger and resentment. The good old days will be missed and confusion and chaos will reign. At the lowest dip of the curve, we come to a point where nothing seems to work any longer and nothing seems to help. When we reach this bottom, all we can do is to let go of the past. As we do this, something starts to change:

we start climbing. The new takes shape and becomes more and more solid. A new reality starts to form; we start experimenting, we feel curiosity. Eventually we decide to embrace the new and enjoy the better version of reality that unfolds for us.

Going through change is not easy. Many organisational change projects fail because change is not managed sufficiently. And in our lives we refuse to embrace the new because of the instinctive fear we have of this initial hard phase.

The key question the change curve asks us is: are you ready to do what it takes? Are you ready to pay the price? And payment in this case is upfront and comes with no money-back guarantee.

I have listened to them for the past three weeks. I have analysed the numbers, I have tested the validity of their hypotheses, I have looked at the trends. I am starting to grow confident that yes, it can be done, and yes, they would be able to do it. And that maybe I could be here, doing it with them. After all, it's been fun to work here for the last three weeks and explore with them various ways in which we can take this small company through an ambitious expansion.

The numbers are there, the opportunity is solid. This is not what I am questioning in my mind. What I am not sure of is if they are ready to do what it takes.

We have talked about the figures, about the pros and the cons; about probabilities and investments. Now it's the time to address the real issue here and I feel apprehensive as I launch myself down this path.

"Are you familiar with the change curve?"

No, they are not. I tell them I feel it's important to talk about this and I ask one of them to Google it.

"Just type in 'change curve'," I say, "and you will find some examples". Actually, there were more than 58 million results on Google last time I checked.

One of them does so and I ask him to pick an image, any image he wants. I don't need to check to see if it helps me make my point. It certainly will. All of the thousands of variants of the change curve deliver the same powerful message.

I ask him to hook his laptop up to the projector and as the change curve shows up on the wall behind me, I start to talk to them about why it looks like this and what it tells us: that it will get worse before it gets better. And about why there's nothing we can do but accept it.

They look at me, unconvinced. This is not the message they were expecting. I carry on with my explanations about how the change the company will have to go through to achieve its ambitious growth targets will disrupt the status quo; will actually negatively impact performance for a while and will lead to frustrations. About why this happens, why it's important that we are all aware of it and we all accept it before we actually decide to do it. And about why I firmly believe it will happen this time too, as it did in every single change project I have managed or been involved with in my twenty years of business experience.

They still look unconvinced. They tell me that maybe it happens to others but it won't happen to them. They look disappointed, as if I am breaking into pieces a long-treasured dream. They look, all of a sudden, unsure that they actually want me to lead this project for them.

I finish with my change curve explanation and I leave it there, hanging on the wall, as I suggest that maybe we should take a few days to think about how we move forward on this.

We end the meeting and switch off the projector, but the change curve is still there with us, its ghost dancing on the wall. To them it's an unlikely possibility they are not prepared to accept. And this, for me, is the sign that I won't take this project further.

Because when one does not want to pay upfront the price of change, it simply won't happen.

Change is tough. It's one of the most stressful situations in our lives and to make it happen we need the commitment to go through with it. It also helps if we expect and prepare for what's coming.

Know that it will be hard for a while as you start to change. Once you decide to go in a different direction, know that this decision will have its price that will need to be paid. Some people in your life might decide to make you change your mind, or they might desert you. Others might change with you. Your routine will not function any longer in a new situation. It will take time to adapt to a new scenario. If you ever dreamt of working in a foreign country, the first weeks once your dream job takes you there will be a far cry from what you had expected. It will be difficult for a while as you settle in, learn how to function in a new society, adapt to a new language. There will be lonely moments to weather and day-to-day challenges you did not have to deal with at home. Know that's part of it. If you made that decision consciously and are convinced it's a good decision for you, just remember that you are travelling on a change curve and you're on the downhill portion. Expect to hit the bottom; a moment when you will question your own decision and have strong doubts that this was a good one. Wait for this to pass and let go of how you imagined things would be. Simply let go and accept the new; let it become part of your life. Get used to it, make friends with it. Maintain a sense of curiosity. See where it takes you. Eventually you will climb out of the change curve. Every single model of it you find on Google will tell you so.

The myth of work–life balance

The work–life balance is one of the biggest buzz phrases of our times, and one of the biggest myths as well. Why? Because when you love what you do there is no such demarcation between 'work' and 'life'. Work becomes life and life becomes work and you flow from one to the other.

How do we do this? By doing what we really love. This sounds simplistic but it's true. To someone passionate about photography, taking pictures will not feel like work. It will not feel like something to dread, to make excuses not to do, to take time off from or devise strategies to do less of. They will actually just want to do it. Same with a painter, a writer, a pianist giving a concert. Entrepreneurs of successful start-ups often work fourteen-hour days for years with no holidays. And they don't complain about it. Their passion keeps them going.

Find where your joy is and it will not feel like work. You might get tired and need a break; you might have days when you don't feel like it, you might have to schedule it to take into account the other things that need to happen in your life. But it will still feel like part of your life.

If you find yourself thinking about work–life balance all the time, you have not got a job that fits in well with your life.

Focus on your strengths

We are all born with a unique set of gifts and talents. It's part of who we are. When we use them, it feels easy. To me writing comes naturally. Putting numbers in spreadsheets does not. If I construct my working life so that I do a lot of writing, my natural talent will help me do this effortlessly. But if I have a job that requires me to put numbers into spreadsheets, I will become irritated, unhappy, and I will be pretty ineffective at doing it.

There is a myth that says we should all train ourselves to be good at everything. I think that's counterproductive. What you are not good at, simply delegate. Choose to do what you are good at. If you are not good with money, there's a limit to how much you can learn if you try to educate yourself. Getting a good financial advisor might be an easier option. If you don't like talking to strangers, don't get a sales job involving cold calls. If you like meeting people, don't get a programming job that will require you to spend hours isolated in front of your computer. If travelling and adapting to new cultures comes easily to you, get a job where this is appreciated. And so on. You get the point.

Don't go against who you are. Accept yourself; respect your gifts and talents. Focus on your strengths. And use them. Your energy will increase the more you use it for the things you are naturally good at and will become depleted the more you force yourself into situations or jobs where you don't naturally fit. Go with the flow, not against it.

When something needs doing, just do it

Nothing stops the energy from flowing more than procrastination. When it becomes clear that something needs to be done, just do it, then and there. Do it and move on. Don't walk around with items hanging off your energy as things you will have to do. Someone popped into your mind and you know you have to speak to that person? Do it now. There is a reason why that person popped into your mind at that moment in time, not later. You pass by a shop and you think "I should remember to come back to buy that here"? Just stop and buy it then and there. Once you are clear about what needs to be done, stop thinking about it – just do it. You read something that touches you and you think that maybe it would be interesting to try out this new yoga class? Go Google it and book a session now. Don't spend time agonising, trying to make the perfect choice. Trust that something arose in you because the perfect moment is now. Go with it, flow with it. Add speed into your life. Glide on your flow.

The quest for power is internal

When you stop looking for power externally, you finally gain it. That's because you have found it within yourself. When you depend on others to feel like you have power, stop and take a look at what is happening. Someone else cannot give you power. You have it within yourself and the only question is how well you access it. This is true for a lot of situations we usually identify with power: the authority to speak up in a meeting, taking responsibility for a project, starting an initiative. Don't walk out there waiting for someone to give you power. Simply consult your internal compass and find out whether the initiative, the comment, the project is part of your path. If it is just do it: make that point, take that responsibility, start that initiative. Go with your internal flow; it will take you where you are supposed to go and it will do so from a position of power. And when you act from your power base, others will instantly recognise this. When you respect your own power, others will respect it too.

Time is what we make of it

So much stress is generated by this one single concept: time. At work our whole life revolves around time. The nine-to-five. The time it takes to prepare for a meeting. Will I make it in time? Time that runs out before a meeting can reach any consensus. Time that is impossible to find in someone's calendar. Time that shrinks incredibly fast when confronted with a looming deadline.

And yet in the middle of all this stress, what is time really made of? Well, it's made of nothing per se: it's just a concept, a socially accepted convention. Someone tells us a report needs to go out tomorrow. We buy into this and we stress like mad to make it happen. I am not saying here that you have to skip deadlines, miss milestones and fail to meet launch dates simply because time does not exist. What I am saying is that sometimes it's helpful to recognise time for what it is: a socially accepted convention. Ask yourself what happens if a deadline is missed: will someone die because of it? In some emergency situations someone actually might, and this deadline will have a completely different weight. But for most cases in our day-to-day jobs, nothing really happens when a deadline is missed. Another one is set and maybe that one will be a little bit more realistic.

When you feel time takes over your life, just remember that your life is real and time is fabricated. Time has no actual power over it. Some people will point out that our own life is made of time, the time we are given between birth and death. I say this is just an illusion. The number of years, months and days we live is just a social convention. Our life is not made up of time, it is made up of living. What have we done with this time? How much have we lived? How deeply have we felt? What energy have we released into the world?

Because in the end, all that matters is what we have contributed to the world. Our actions, our thoughts, our wishes, all that we have been and are, are constantly releasing energy into the world. And the effect of that energy will still be here, long after we are gone. The examples we set, the legacy we left, the way we educated our children, the houses we built, the companies we constructed, the art we created. All these things stay here long after we are gone and touch the lives of many more people than we can possibly imagine.

So live your life well, fill it with authentic and real living. Forget about the stress of time, of deadlines.

Because in the end, time is only what we make of it.

What makes sense is often the best way forward

In our work life, we focus so much on applying the models and frameworks we have acquired during the long years of our education that we sometimes forget the basic decision-making technique mankind had available for ages: common sense.

No matter what your tools and models tell you, no matter the result of a complicated analysis, it needs to make sense. Common sense. For you and for everyone else involved. Because when it only makes sense for one party at the table and it does not make sense to the other party, it does not make sense as a whole. Hence, it simply does not make sense. This is another way to look at the win–win concept.

When you look at alternatives and choose where to direct your energy, ask yourself this simple but powerful question: does it make sense? For you, for the others, for everyone involved. Is this in the best interests of everyone? Does this make sense as a whole? If it does not, leave it there.

We have been trying to nail down this deal for ages. We are four people around a table and we have already been in discussions for a few hours. We have revised the pros and cons, we have discussed and re-discussed every single detail, checked if we can make it better.

We all want it. We have taken all this time to look at everything because we all want it. In our minds it ticks some boxes, enough boxes to make us want it. It looks like a good enough deal. Yes, there are some parts we have still not found answers for but hey, we could make it work.

And yet the deal is still there on the table after all these hours and all these meetings. It is there, scribbled on the white sheets of paper, in the drawings we have made, in our attempt to cover each point. It is there in the glasses of water half drunk. It floats away in the air of that meeting room, which starts to feel stuffy after four hours of negotiations.

It is there with us and looks back at us with tired eyes. It is trying to talk to us but we do not listen, too busy to push and tweak and make all the details fit so that we can finally sign on the dotted line and go home with a done deal.

And then I get it. I suddenly get it as I look absent-mindedly at all the papers with our scribbling on that have been left in the middle of the table.

"I think this deal does not want to go anywhere..." I say slowly.

They look at me with a mixture of irritation and relief. They feel it too. We had been trying hard but it simply does not make a lot of sense.

We leave it there, in that room, on that table, where it wants to stay. We leave it where it makes sense that it remains. We leave it and move on, and we are all much better off for having done so.

Direct your energy to create joy

Following your passions will always give you a good indication as to where your path lies. In Chapter 5 we explored how to tap into the power that our passions give us access to. As we direct our energy to manifest the life that we want, it is important to keep these passions in mind. They are here with us because they ask to be lived. As we make space for them, as we incorporate them into the things we attract in our lives and make decisions for, they will become part of our flow. They will increase the speed and the ease with which we glide.

Incorporating passions into our work will make it smoother, richer, more internally rewarding. It will increase our energy. This does not necessarily mean that we have to convert our passions into work. Sometimes passions are there simply to complement a work situation. But by always incorporating as much as we can from the things we truly care about, feel passionate about or which give us energy into the activities we do for 'work', we will increase the joy we bring to our lives.

Our passions are there to help us experience joy. When we do so, we create things that bring joy to others. In turn they connect to their inner joy, and this helps them discover their own passions and pursue them. It's a circle and in the end, incorporating passions into our lives means we bring joy into the world.

When you need a little help

We are part of the world. As such, our energy system is constantly interconnected with the energy system of everything around us. At any given point in time, there are powerful forces shaping the reality around us. It helps if we are aware of these trends so that we can harness their power and flow with them instead of against them. A few of them are listed below:

Astrology

Astrology is one of the oldest sciences on earth. It's been traced back to at least the second millennium BC and it has been used for centuries to study the position of celestial bodies and predict their effect on human actions. All major civilisations on Earth had their own form of astrology: the Indians and the Chinese in Asia, the Mayans and Aztecs in America. It has reached Europe, coming from Mesopotamia through Ancient Greece, through Rome and the Arab world. Throughout the Middle Ages, it was widely used at all royals courts in Europe.

Astrology can give us powerful indicators as to when our actions will be helped by the bigger trends and when they will not. Some of those are very relevant to our day-to-day working lives. Some of the astrological movements will affect everyone and some will apply to each of us individually, according to the time and place of our birth. For instance, planets have retrograde phases: that is, moments when their trajectory appears to go backwards. These phases are moments of low energy. Each planet in our solar system also governs some specific things. Take Mercury, for instance. This planet governs technology, travel and communication, among other things. If a scheduled launch date for unveiling new technology happens to take place during a Mercury retrograde phase, there will be a much higher probability than usual of something going wrong with that launch or the way the technology functions. Similarly, travel will be impacted negatively and any communication will become difficult. If we know when these Mercury retrograde periods happen within the year (they happen about four times a year), we can build this into our schedules and take precautions. A Mercury retrograde transit will affect everyone, although some individuals will be more impacted than others.

On the other hand, your date and time of birth will give you a map of celestial bodies that will project a certain influence on you. If you know how and when these impacts will be felt most strongly, you can use this energy to your advantage rather than going against it.

If you want to use this tool, it pays to arrange a session with a professional. The daily, weekly and monthly horoscopes published by media tend to be just for entertainment purposes.

The moon's phases

The moon touches all forms of life on Earth. It makes oceans move with tides, it affects plants and animals. Farmers knew about this for centuries and used the phases of the moon as reliable indicators for when to plant, to prune or to harvest. For us, aligning our actions to the phases of the moon means we will tap into its enormous power and use it to move forward.

The new moon, when you can't see it at all, is a great time to complete and prepare. Look to close down what remained from the previous moon cycle and prepare for the new one. Think about your intentions. Draw your plans. Put the past to rest. Renew, just as the moon does.

When the moon is waxing – that is, when it gradually increases its presence in the sky – it's the ideal time for new beginnings. Start new projects, take the first steps in implementing your plans, develop new routines. Sign up for a gym, start a detox regime. Start writing a new book. As the moon rises in the sky, so do our energy levels. Go with this flow: stretch, grow, increase, expand.

When the moon is at its fullest, it's the time for maximum expression. Hold important meetings now. Enjoy your greatest parties and social events. Plan your important presentations, unveil your new products. Energy reaches its peak here, creativity booms, intuition is powerful. Enjoy and celebrate.

When the moon starts shrinking and goes into the 'waning' phase, the energy will gradually diminish. It's time to tie in loose ends, turn inwards, complete and get ready to let go. It's a good time to finalise projects, complete tasks, wrap up things, declutter, let go of the past.

Numerology

Numerology is the study of numbers and of the energy they bring into our life. Some credit Pythagoras, the ancient Greek mathematician, as the founder of this science; others trace it back to the Hebrew Kabbalah. Throughout the centuries, it has been used extensively to predict auspicious times for a variety of actions. Our date of birth will have significance, as will all numbers that are important in our lives. They will tell us, for instance, when we are governed by an 'ending' period, and it may not be the best time to start something new then. They will tell us when we reach the key points in our lives, and ideal periods for major moves and decisions. As with everything else, you may choose to believe in it or you may not, but know that it is there in case you feel inclined to consult it.

Feng shui

Feng shui is a traditional Chinese system for harmonising the energy of the environment with your personal energy. It can help with choosing, arranging and decorating your home and your office to increase the speed at which you manifest your intentions. It takes into account a complex system of auspicious directions, forms of landscape and placement of objects and it looks at how the energy of objects interacts with other objects, and with the person living there. Its goal is to keep the energy flowing in harmony and therefore add to the energy of the people living or working in that environment. There are many feng shui practitioners practising in almost every country, and you can easily find them through an Internet search.

Rituals

A ritual represents a conscious connection between an intention and an actual deed. Writing your intentions down, or burning a piece of paper on which you have written what you want to let go of, are examples of rituals you can perform to help with directing your energy.

A moon phase ritual can be used to harvest the power of the moon phases. Write down a few intentions for the month ahead on a new moon day. Revise them on the full moon day, see where you are and what still needs to happen. Then look at them again next time the moon is new and see what you should let go of and what you should keep for the month ahead. Other people write their intentions on a list on new moon day and burn the list on full moon day two weeks later as a form of releasing the intentions into the universe. Or plant actual seeds in their garden on new moon day and assign one intention to each seed.

Rituals are highly personalised and we each have our own small rituals, whether we pay attention to them or not. Establishing conscious rituals to work with your energy will give this habit a place of importance into your life and this in itself will raise the vibration of your energy.

Summary: How to direct your energy to manifest the life that you want

- Cultivate your ability to attract and receive.
- Maintain your high energy vibration and correct any limiting beliefs.
- Find the state of flow and let yourself flow with it.
- As your intentions start turning into reality, remember to keep them effortless, clear, open, simple, honest and playful. Then let them go.
- Live in the present. Let go of the past and don't try to anticipate the future.
- Programme your aura to constantly attract what is good for you and repel what is negative.
- Honour what arises in you and express your truth.
- Find your point of optimum Return to Scale and stick to it.
- Develop your BATNA and be happy with it.
- Accept to pay the price for change upfront.
- Turn work–life balance into work that fits naturally within your life.
- Focus on your strengths not on your weaknesses.
- Look for power internally and act from that power base.
- Remember, time is what you make of it.
- Incorporate common sense into your decisions and actions.
- Consciously direct your energy to create joy.
- Be aware of how larger energy systems impact your life.

Direction-setting Exercises:

> **6.1 Practise visually attracting what you want to manifest in your life:**

- Sit comfortably, ground, cleanse and protect your energy. Open your chakras.

- Imagine the edge of your aura turning into a very powerful magnet.

- Set the intention that this magnet will repel all that is bad for you and attract all that is good for you.

- Tune into it and actually feel the enormous power of attraction it has.

- Now imagine something you want to attract to your life.

- Visualise the powerful attraction that your aura sends out towards the object of your desires.

- Visualise it coming to you, entering your aura, entering your body and settling into your heart.

- Say "I receive it." Say "Thank you."

- Then ground it, send it deep down through your roots to the centre of the earth and imagine planting it there.

- Visualise how it takes root and grows from there. You can see it growing as a tree, a plant, a flower or anything you like.

- Do this one by one with everything you want to attract to your life.

- Then form an intention that this magnet repels anything that is negative for you, anything that lowers your vibration. Visualise it sending away negative energy and hold the intention that everything that is sent away is transmuted into positive energy for the universe.

- At the end, say "Thank you" again.

- Close your chakras, check your grounding, open your eyes and carry on with your day.

A word of warning: never do these exercises imagining you are attracting a specific person into your life. If you want love, imagine this as a concept entering your heart, not as a person that you know. If you desire friends, imagine this as a general concept, or as faceless and nameless friends entering your life. Don't send your attraction power out there to Mary, John or Bob. Respect other people's free will and energy, and know that trying to interfere with their energy is a form of manipulation and it will have serious negative consequences for you and for them. Never imagine manipulating other people's energy for any purpose, including when you are absolutely convinced it is in their or your best interests. The only time you can work with someone else's energy is if they give you their express permission to do so and ask for your help, or you are doing it for your child who is still dependent on you.

7.

Reflect: Take time to assess, assimilate and course correct

Living consciously is a lifetime commitment. It does not happen overnight. It takes time to build. It also takes commitment to maintain, to assess and to continuously improve. Raising our vibrations and the quality of the energy we send out into the world is a never-ending exercise. The more we learn, the more we realise how much there is to learn. The more we heal, the more further levels of required healing reveal themselves; the more we understand, the fuller our life becomes, and with that new borders are crossed, new horizons revealed, new challenges tackled.

First, we need to increase our energy to the level required to be able to manifest. We do this by grounding, cleansing and protecting our energy. We also do it by tapping into our power sources, learning which of our actions, habits or environments increase it and which ones decrease it. We make healthy choices. We connect and listen to our inner voice. Then we reach a point when things start to flow into our lives easily. We accept this flow and we glide with it. We make the right decisions, the ones that arise effortlessly from the sea of our internal *knowledge*, we take the first steps without worrying about the next ones, we differentiate between truth and illusions, myths and reality. We attract, we receive, we honour what comes up in us and we move forward.

All this is a lifelong process. It never stops. To make it meaningful, though, we also need to take the time to look at it, to assess the results we get, to assimilate the lessons that we are given, to correct our inevitable mistakes.

The dictionary defines 'reflect' as taking time to think deeply or carefully about something. About what worked and what did not. What increased my energy and what decreased it. When I did well and how I can do better.

Taking time to reflect is a state, not an action specifically determined in time. Reflect when you become aware you need to, when something out there triggers questions; reflect continuously and consciously. Understand what is happening, see the effects of your actions, decisions, intentions. See the results of your increased energy.

Principles of reflection

There are four key principles that can help us understand where we are on this reflection journey:

Responsibility

Most of us are comfortable with the concept of responsibility for our own words or deeds. Some of us will even be comfortable with the notion of taking responsibility for all that we attract into our lives. And yet there is another layer.

The Hawaiian people take responsibility very seriously. They have an ancient tradition of reconciliation and forgiveness that actually makes a person responsible for everything. For absolutely everything that happens in his life and for everyone he crosses paths with. It sounds strange but it's amazingly effective. It's called *ho'oponopono* and the root of the word means 'to put right, to correct, to adjust, arrange, rectify or tidy up'. It works like this: for every situation we encounter in our lives, we turn inwards and say: "I love you. I'm sorry. Please forgive me. Thank you." If someone does something bad to you, say this. If you witness someone struggling, even if you are not connected to their struggle, say this. If you are ill, say this. If someone you love is going through problems, say this. Say this for everything and for everyone. Basically take responsibility for this thing that shows up in your life, in whatever shape or form it appears. Believe it is there because you are responsible for it in some mysterious and incomprehensible way. Accept this responsibility without questioning it. Just say: "I love you. I'm sorry. Please forgive me. Thank you." And then do so again.

One amazing result of this technique was achieved by a psychologist at a state hospital in Hawaii, who cured a full ward of criminally insane patients without ever seeing any of them. What did he actually do? He said "I am sorry" and I" love you". Did he say it to them? No, he said it to himself. He actually sent forgiveness and love to his own self, to that part inside him that resonated with what was happening outside. He did that consistently for a long period of time. And that had the effect of changing the reality around him. It sounds like science fiction but the case is well-documented.

We are used to thinking of responsibility as limited to that which we do ourselves. This technique teaches us that our responsibility extends far further than this. Everything that shows up in our life, including the people who wrong us, is there because, in a way, we have created it. We are the creators of our own universe. And as such, the more we heal, the more the world around us heals. As a philosophical concept many of us can probably relate to this, but when expressed in this kind of extreme responsibility technique most of us might shake our heads in doubt.

And yet what have you got to lose? If something bad happens around you or to you, simply turn inside and say in your mind "I love you. I'm sorry. Please forgive me. Thank you." No one needs to know about this. Try it out and see what happens.

If you can entertain this idea, even if for only a few minutes, you can see what amazing new perspectives it can create. We are responsible for our lives. OK, we get that. No, not just that. We are responsible for *all* our lives. For *everything* that shows up in our lives. For the bad economy. For the beggar we pass by in the street. For the man who robbed us at gunpoint. For the lover who broke our heart. For the boss who bullied us.

For the friend who let us down. This is far harder to accept, but simply being open to this idea will bring though a whole new perspective. And no, it has nothing to do with guilt. Responsibility is not guilt. Guilt is a low vibration emotion that weighs us down. Responsibility empowers us. Because if we accept we are responsible for something, we also accept we have the power to change it.

We are responsible for everything and at the same time we are responsible for nothing. Responsibility is not a limited concept, something that can be parcelled, divided up and shared. You simply take it. For whatever shows up in your life.

Take it without guilt, without self-punishment. Take it simply as it comes. Go inside yourself, to the very place that is touched by something happening in the outside world. Go there and give yourself love and forgiveness. It will heal you. And then the life around you will heal too.

Authenticity

When we are not aware of or connected to our internal power, we are not really ourselves. At the same time, living out of touch with ourselves prevents us from accessing our own power. The two are interconnected: one cannot exist without the other. Sounds simplistic but think about it: if you are trying to constantly be someone else in order to please someone, to escape from something, to obtain something or for whatever other reason, how can that someone else have access to your power? That someone else you are trying to be, the persona you are building, is not real. It will not have a reservoir of personal power to tap into. It will have to rely on getting some power from others, and this might come from pleasing them or from being admired by them. This energy influx will be a poor substitute for the real power base that remains untapped.

When we are not authentic, we are weak. To maintain an image or a mask we spend incredible amounts of energy, because this image or mask is not naturally anchored into our power base. We have to constantly work at maintaining it.

Being authentic, on the other hand, is effortless. It comes naturally to us to be who we are. So then what happens that prevents us from being true to ourselves?

We may care too much about what others say or think about us. If we are not fully within ourselves, if we leave a little piece of us inside the heads of everyone we want to please and try to assess ourselves through their eyes, our energy is not fully home. We are not grounded. It is very difficult to be grounded and not be authentic. If you want to check how authentic you are in a given situation, check your grounding.

Or maybe we don't want to hurt the feelings of others so we refrain from being fully ourselves, from saying what we think or doing what we feel is right for us. For a while, we achieve our purpose: we don't hurt them. We hurt our own selves instead, and as a result we lose energy. We then struggle to keep the mask we have created and we lose even more energy. Then we end up depleted quite quickly and when there is no more energy to spend on trying to keep the mask on, we lose it anyway and revert back to who we are naturally. Which hurts the very same person we initially tried to avoid hurting. Except that in the meantime, we have depleted ourselves too. Not really worth it.

I'm not saying it's good to be insensitive to the feelings of others. By all means, find a compassionate way to express what you need to express and then live your truth. If you don't do it you will end up hurting them anyway, and hurting yourself too.

Integrity

Integrity is defined as the state of being complete or whole. It comes from the Latin word 'integer', which means whole. We are living in a state of integrity when we have access to all of ourselves; when we are whole. When we have called our energy home, we have grounded, cleansed and protected our energy.

Integrity is also defined as having moral principles. It's not about having or not having them. All people are born with them. Moral principles are the expression of universal energy. The trouble is that not all people have access to them, just as not all of us fully have access to our power base. Once we rebuild these bridges within ourselves, integrity comes to us automatically. One cannot have full access to his or her own energy, feel their full power base and not live with integrity. Once we are back in touch with the whole of who we are, this wholeness lives through us and expresses through us continuously.

Honesty

Something happens in us when we speak the truth. Our energy perceives the energy of truth and alights upon it. It gets a boost. Whereas the energy of non-truth is a depletion of the universal energy. When we lie, our energy goes down. When we live a lie, we will have to spend huge amounts of energy to fuel that lie. It is as simple as that. Telling the truth will increase your energy. Living your truth will multiply it. Not doing so will decrease it.

All cultures in the world have some sort of a confession ritual. In the Catholic world, it's about confessing your sins to a priest who will then pray for your forgiveness. For the Vanuatu people in South Pacific, confession is the therapy for any illness. They believe that secrecy gives power to illnesses. Once the error is confessed, it holds no further power over that person. Rather it releases the personal power of that person to assist them with healing.

Confession is the remedy for those times when we have lived out of truth. This, together with the intention to live the truth from that moment onwards, will take us back to our power every time.

These four principles are the backbone of living consciously. When in doubt, check against these principles. It sounds simple, and it can actually be that simple. Whenever we deviate from our path, one of these four principles will start beaming red alert lights. If we pay attention and we welcome the message, we can use it to correct our course and get back on track.

Why do we need to deviate, you may wonder? Why is it that once we have tapped into our power base, we still lose the course? Why can it not all be a simple straight line?

Because straight lines are boring: they don't create beauty as they flow. A butterfly does not fly in straight lines, it dances. As it does so, it creates beauty. A shoal of fish does not move in straight lines; birds don't fly in straight lines either. Fish adjust to the current in the water, birds account for the wind. A boat that sails from A to B will do so in a series of zigzag moves. It will never be a straight line. There are very few straight lines in nature. And ultimately, even when we do find them, it's an illusion, because a straight line on a spherical earth is always going to be curved.

We don't move in straight lines because if we did we would lose all the beauty of exploration and adventure that comes with drifting from the straight path. We would be poorer for it, and our time on earth would be so much sadder. We would lose opportunities to stumble upon discoveries, to appreciate beauty in different ways; we would miss the chances to connect with what we did not even think existed.

Go ahead: make mistakes, take your time and lose your way. It's the best thing you can do for yourself. When you need to come back and find true north again, reflect on these four principles: they will bring you home. And then wander off your path and explore the side roads again, see them for what they are, pursue your illusions, which sometimes you might confuse with dreams, and see where they end: in a puff of smoke usually. Then find a trace of something else, of something solid, of a real dream that might be covered in mud at first. Check it out. Clean it up, bring it into the sunlight. See if it's just a piece of mud or if there might be a gem hiding in there. Take your time and make your mistakes. Dance without reason and lose your way. And when you are done exploring the forest around you, call your principles to guide you home.

It's all part of being human.

The myths of reflection

Just as those four pillars of truth will always guide us home, there will be a myriad of illusions, of myths that people have created, that will make us lose our way. Both the indicators of true north and the lure of illusion are necessary if we are to lose our way once in a while so as to be able to find it again.

Know them for what they are. Recognise them when they come to you, when they try to lure you away with their seductive power. Know them even when you give in and follow them. And even if you lose your way to them, at least you will have done it consciously.

Here are the most common ones:

The trap of feedback

The corporate world loves feedback. It's a buzzword and it is used in countless theories on how to increase your self-awareness. Ask for feedback, they say. Reflect on what you get back. Take constructive criticism. Adjust your behaviours. Constantly check how you are perceived… and so on.

While there might be some value in receiving feedback, there are also many pitfalls for watch out for. And that's because feedback given to you by other people will always reflect the energy of those other people, whether consciously or unconsciously. Let's look at the conscious part first:

- People you ask for feedback might not have your best interests at heart. They may envy you or hold a grudge and use this opportunity for revenge, or try to sabotage you because it benefits them. They will do so by trying to lower your self-esteem, your self-confidence, your power. They will do so by giving you negative feedback. Why do they need to do that? Because when you have low self-esteem, low self-confidence and low personal power, you are easier to manipulate or control. You may stay in a job that pays less than you should earn. You may take over tasks that are not yours to do and complete them for someone else. You may put up with abusive behaviour. And the list goes on. At work, feedback is often used as a weapon or threat. Negative feedback is disguised under layers of positive feedback, but its core purpose is to gain easy access to another person's psyche in order to facilitate manipulation.

- People might need a justification for their actions. When you get laid off by a company, there will always be negative feedback that will go with that. Just know it for what it is. Your boss or the boss of your boss needs a reason why you are being let go. Whether it is true or not, is not the question here.

The unconscious part of the feedback you receive from people is much broader and much more fascinating. People will always pour their own beliefs and strategies about how life should be into the feedback they give you: to an ordered person, someone who is not as ordered will be something to correct, to deal with. Hence negative feedback: you need to be more ordered. To someone who has never dared to live their full life potential, the choices of a person who dares to do so seem foolish, risky and irresponsible. Their feedback will inevitably reflect that, since it's given from their point of view. Others will pour all their deep sadness, transformed into envy, into the feedback or advice they give you: "don't quit your job, it will ruin your career," they say, but they think "I wish I was able to do what she does."

Feedback from a low-vibration person will be useless to a person with a higher energy vibration. This is because the person whose energy is still low cannot fully comprehend the person whose energy is stronger; they have no access to that type of energy yet. Hence inevitably their feedback will try to 'pull back' the person with higher energy to make them fit into their limited vision of the world.

Feedback from people continuously stuck in 'trying to help' mode is even more dangerous. This is because most of these people are subconsciously trying to help themselves. They do so by constantly projecting their own issues and difficulties on to others around them and then trying to fix them. When you come across this, know it for what it is: a projection.

Feedback from other people rarely works because it will be full of those other people's stuff. When asking for feedback, maintain your awareness that some of the stuff you get back will have nothing to do with you. If you forget about this, you run the risk of being too open to others' energy and this gives your power away.

So what is the solution? To walk through life stubbornly refusing to listen to any type of feedback? Not really. There is one type of feedback that is useful, but this one does not come from other people

The real feedback in our lives will come from life itself. If whatever we do benefits our energy, if we feel more real, more alive, more in touch with ourselves as a result of what we are doing, it means we are doing well. If we feel more depleted, less authentic, more ill and we are getting worse results, we are not doing well. It's as simple as that. The results in our life will speak for themselves. The amount of 'struggle' we experience will give us an indication as to where we are. A quick check on where we are with those four principles and on the results we are getting is enough. If they point north, trust that compass. It is far more accurate than what other people may think of you.

So what do we do with all this feedback we are inundated with in corporate environments? What do we do with the performance reviews, with the personal development plans, with the 'here's what you need to improve' type of recommendations?

We take them for what they are: a mix of other people's conscious or unconscious attempts to interfere with our energy. We ground, cleanse and protect our energy and then we look at what comes to us and we divide it into a few buckets.

The first bucket is for things we simply throw out. We don't need to spend too much time thinking about it. If Auntie Jolie thinks I should get married instead of travelling the world and if what I truly desire right now is to travel the world, I shouldn't concern myself with what Auntie Jolie thinks.

The second bucket will be filled with feedback related to the work that we do. Let's say I get told I need to be more detail-oriented at work. I am normally not a detail-oriented person, I am a big-picture person. So what I am getting told is that I am in the wrong job for my strengths.

As I take some time to think about how to deal with this, I find that I can:

1. Change my job immediately.

2. Stick with my job for a while and see if the increased detail-oriented feature is something I can sort out. I can spend some energy trying to do that for a while or find creative ways around it. Maybe I can hire an assistant who is detail-oriented and have that person cover for my lack of that skill. Or maybe I can ask for different projects that will require less attention to detail...; or

3. I can actually try to become a detail-oriented person even though this is not who I really am. Doing this will deplete my energy because it goes against who I am. I can train myself to be ok with it for a while, but it will never be my natural strength so I will commit myself to a path of mediocrity. I will never excel at it. I will spend a lot of energy trying to 'fix' something perceived as a weakness in me instead of flying with my strengths. Not a winning strategy.

The third bucket is for the things we have heard and that have touched us. We might have asked for feedback or it may have come to us unexpectedly, but something that we have heard has touched us. First of all we need to check if it is real. Where did the feedback come from? Did it come from a person whose energy is as high or higher than ours? Not higher in absolute comparisons, because everyone's energy is unique, but in terms of how much they are in touch with their power base. If it comes from a higher vibration, it may actually be beneficial for us. Then we need to check what exactly it touched inside us. Did it hit my insecurities? My self-doubt? My guilt? What was my energy response when it touched me? Did my body contract? Did my energy go down? If any of these symptoms are present, the feedback is actually touching a point of illusion or trauma inside me. It's not real. It does not touch the core of my truth. It only touches some points or little pockets of unconsciousness in me. It points me to what I still need to work with inside me; to heal. If this is the case, the best I can do is to use the feedback to do some work on those aspects I need to heal. I can do this through meditation, visualisation, the ho'oponopono technique, through talking to a therapist or whatever takes my fancy. I spend some time with this issue and see what inside of me needs to be healed.

And then there is a fourth bucket. This is for feedback that has touched a chord inside and that feels real. I have checked and it's not touching a place of fear, of contraction, but a place of opening, of relaxation, of expansion. A place of Truth. I hear it and I have neither good nor bad feelings. I hear it and I know it's true. I may not know how exactly it is true but I recognise the vibration of truth. Some feedback that initially fell into the third bucket, i.e. that generated a strong emotional response in me initially, can actually belong here as well. That's because once the initial emotion it stirred is settled, we recognise it as true. Whether the vibration of truth comes to us immediately or after a while, know that it always points to valuable feedback. And this is the only type of feedback worth keeping and committing to working on.

He had asked for feedback as soon as I had started the new assignment. He had asked less than a week into it, when all I had done was read materials and say hi to people. He had asked everyone who I had interacted with what they thought about me and he had done this more than a few times. People tried to be polite and said, "She seems nice." There was nothing more they could say about me. I smiled when I met them, we exchanged a few words and that was it. They had hired me to lead a big initiative and they trusted they had made the right decision to hire me. And they knew I wouldn't be able to do that overnight because I needed time to learn and digest what this was all about. I was busy climbing up my learning curve and they respected this.

But he was not patient. He wanted reassurance, immediate and constant reassurance. He was the director of the intermediary company that had placed me with this client. He wanted to make sure I would do a good job on this project and he wanted this reassurance even before I had actually started to do anything.

He asked again by the time I got to the second week. I started to sense that the people I was working with were watching me with some surprise. "If she really knows what she is doing, why has he asked so many times what we think about her?" I read in their minds. He was lowering his credibility and mine too, but unaware of what he was doing, he was going on and on and on, constantly asking for feedback.

Then he asked me for feedback on how I thought I was doing. I told him I had no time to think about it because I was busy ramping up, getting ready to actually do something. I told him to relax, to trust. He wouldn't; he couldn't.

He carried on asking for feedback every week until someone snapped at him in the middle of a conference call. "She's doing well," he said. "I already told you so. And we should not have this conversation if front of her anyway." I kept quiet during the call but I felt the irritation starting to bubble up in me.

He was doing this to try to lower my power. Subconsciously, of course. He was transmitting a message of "I don't trust her," and this message in the minds of the people I worked with was going to make my task more difficult. He was effectively and seriously sabotaging me.

But there was no way he could see this. He behaved in that way because of the deep pit of self-doubt he carried within himself. He had a great need for constant reassurance and no matter how much of it he got in the actual world, it would not make him stop. It came from deep within his wounded self.

I carried on with my project. People learned to trust me. It just took a little longer than usual because I had to recover from the doubt his behaviour had generated. The project went well. I connected to my internal power and the client started to perceive this. Slowly, we moved past the drama of excessive feedback.

And then, as we got to the end of the project, it came back to bite me once more.

"I have asked everyone you worked with to send me their feedback about you. We can meet and talk about the results of this exercise if you like," he said.

"No we won't," I thought. Because that feedback wouldn't be useful to me. I already knew how I'd done on that project. I knew it from a mixture of the results I'd got, the atmosphere I'd created, my intuition and my one-to-one connections with the very same people he had asked for a formal evaluation from. I had already learned my own lessons from the project, I knew what worked and what did not: I didn't need to send a survey out for this. And his useless formal feedback exercise at the end of it served one purpose only: to lower the energy again. To lower his energy as it tapped into the same need-for-reassurance place it originally came from. And to lower my energy and make me more 'manageable' on a future project in case I let it touch me.

And as we finished the project on the same theme we started with, I understood one more thing: his need to ask for constant feedback was an expression of his issues.

My irritation with this was an expression of mine. And I realised that I had better work with that irritation to see what was hiding in there, and that maybe I should learn to accept the unconsciousness of others with grace.

And so the feedback I never wanted became feedback in itself for me.

The myth of helping others

A preoccupation with helping others and saving the world rarely achieves anything. That's because, paradoxically, we are all the same, and yet at the same time we are all different. The principles of truth are the same for each of us, the laws by which our personal energy increases or decreases are the same for everyone. However, everyone is different in their approach, their outlook, their understanding. We all have our unique personality, our unique blueprint. And yet we are all part of the same energy.

What does this mean? It means that the only person you can truly help is yourself. Once you do this, the light that you radiate will be sufficient to help other people. It will do so effortlessly, and most importantly without you having to push to achieve it. Once you push, you lower your vibration and it will no longer be able to effectively help other people. The only way you can help is by not trying to help.

When you feel the drive to help or to fix someone or something, look inside. Look at the aspect in you that needs helping. Stop projecting your own issues on to the world and trying to fix them though others. Look inside yourself and see what is in need of healing right now. Once you find it, focus on that, not on its manifestation in the outside world.

Remember, life talks to us. A situation that needs rescuing in the outside world points to something in us. This is where the actual need for healing lies.

I am not saying you should ignore a person who's drowning or that you have to pass through life as an insensitive and careless egomaniac. On the contrary. When something crosses your path, it's there for a reason. Don't think too much about it, just do the obvious. Use your common sense. If actions arise in you, trust them. But do them without the obsessive intention to *help*. Instead, focus on spreading light, joy and good energy around you as you walk on your path. If someone asks you for advice, give it as it comes, don't think too much about it. Answer the question that is asked of you. If someone asks for your help, help if you can. There's nothing wrong with that. But if someone does not ask for your advice or help, refrain from giving it. If you don't it will be wasted, and this is the best-case scenario. In the worst-case scenario, you will end up harming the very person you are trying to help because you give them something they are not yet ready to receive. The best thing you can do for the people around you is to respect them and send them love. When actions arise in you, it's best to check where they come from. If they come from a place of truth, honour them. If they come from a place of personal projection, go deeper and search for where in there the truth lies.

Also, there is a fundamental difference between charity and sharing abundance. Charity encourages dependency, disempowers people and is often done with the purpose of masking deep wounds within the psyche of the giver or getting energy from the very people it is aimed at 'helping'. Sharing abundance, on the other hand, comes effortlessly, rises naturally, empowers people and increases the energy of everyone concerned. When you give, check which place you give from and if doing this will raise or lower the energy of the receiver. If you turn inside to check, your heart will always tell you the truth. Share your abundance on a daily basis as it comes to you. Do this by sharing love, by writing a book, by giving gifts, by creating positive experiences for yourself and others. Share the energy that arises in you by letting it flow freely. When it does, others around you will be able to use it to help cast light on their own shadows and increase their energy in the process. As you let it flow, know that this is the only thing you can do for others. And that it is enough.

The illusion of being alone

We have all been conditioned to think we are alone. It happened mainly during our education. It started when we were babies and the modern living arrangements in the Western world meant we very likely had our own room where we were left alone to sleep and play, which accounted for more than half of our lives at that age. It continued in school, when we were awarded grades and told to study alone, to compete with others. It carried on through our working lives. We have our individual desks, our own job description, and our personal computer. We are supposed to do our jobs. We are expected to cope with whatever comes up, deal with it and move on. Alone, most of the time.

And yet we are not alone. Once we allow ourselves to feel and live the constant flow of life in us, once we allow our energy to carry us where we are meant to go, we realise that there are others on our path who are there to help us. There are those who show up as our schoolfriends when we are seven and stay with us throughout our lives. There are mentors who show up as if by magic when we need them, therapists that you hear about when you set the intention to heal. Friends who live a life of authenticity and show you it's possible for you to do that too. Couples who have great marriages, and when you fail at every single relationship you attempt, they are there in your life to show you that it can be done. There are passions that come to support you, and there are invisible guides all around you who can help and direct you if you just believe they can.

Life flows all around us and we are never alone. When in need, we can tap into this huge reservoir of help constantly and naturally available to us. Set an intention and it will be answered. It really works as simply as that. On two conditions though: the first is that you keep the intention alive in you for the time it takes to actually come true. And the second is that you let it come the way it wants.

Life will give us the answers in the most creative and unusual ways. If we are open to them, we will receive them. If we are locked into prejudices, a desperate need for control or applying over and over again the same old patterns, we will miss these opportunities; we will miss the answers. We will then ask again, and the answers will come back again to us, and we will miss them once again if we don't allow ourselves to be open.

Help is all around us. Just ask for it and be open to receiving it when it comes, in whatever way it comes.

Healthy support does not create dependency. It will come when it's required and it will stay with you for a while. Then it will leave, and when it does, it is important that you let it go. Just like you use a crutch for six weeks after you break a bone and then you no longer need it, letting go of a support that served you well for a while becomes key in your journey to recovery. Don't hold on to the crutch for the rest of your life. Similarly, don't hold on to a therapy or support mechanism once you no longer need it. Learn to identify this point, accept the *knowledge* when it comes, and let it go. It will go so that another type of support can show up in your life. Something that is more suitable to where you are now; the type of issues you have to deal with now. True support grows and evolves constantly, just like we do.

Beware of the world of therapists, coaches and professional helpers who cling on to you because you are a source of income, or a source of personal validation, or because they have projected on to you their own internal issues and are trying to fix those. Beware of carrying them in your life longer than needed. Look for the support you need for a specific issue and time in your life. Welcome it when it comes and use it well, then let it go and walk alone for a while. See what comes next.

And then there is another type of support that frequently crosses our path. When we meet someone in our lives and that meeting touches us profoundly, we are likely to have met the same energy we carry, reflected in someone else. The popular description for this type of encounter is a soulmate connection. Romantic movies and novels have tended to interpret this as a romantic union and taken it into 'happily ever after' territory. But this is not necessarily the case.

You will have many soulmates, not just one, and they will show up throughout your life in a variety of shapes and forms. Soulmates are not only the people you fall in love with. Soulmates are all the people who touch you profoundly. They could be a mentor at work, a friend you shared your school years with and with whom you have remained in constant contact, although you may have been on completely different paths, for many years afterwards. Your purpose in each other's lives might be to simply meet a couple of times a year and witness the other's path. These encounters will fill you both with a feeling of deep joy and you will feel the truth of that connection.

Soulmates show up at difficult points in your life, and sometimes all they do is give you a message which helps you reframe the aspect of reality you are struggling with. And then they leave. At other times they show up when you feel you cannot do things by yourself. They sit with you for a while and just by sitting there, next to you, they help you navigate the part of your path you are struggling with. And then they go.

Or they might show up as a total stranger at a party, but there is something about him, something in his eyes perhaps, and no, it's not romantic, and no, it's not a good networking connection either, but there's something about that person, something impossible to know and difficult to describe; something that tells you that you have met them before, you know them and they know you and you have something for each other. And then you keep in touch simply because of that something, that unclear sensation floating in the air. And then they bring other people or events into your life and they happen to be exactly what you need at the time. And they may stay on to witness how you do with what they brought you, or they may vanish like they have never been there.

At other times they show up as impossible encounters, strong connections which shoot up for a brief moment, and you know you will never see them again. You may wonder what the purpose of that encounter was and you may never find out. Maybe it happened just so that you could say hello to someone you had met before. And then to say goodbye, immediately afterwards. And the extremely short duration of that encounter does not take away any of the immense depth that you sense in it. Even if only for a moment, you know you have met a soulmate.

Soulmates are all around us. Sometimes we marry them. Sometimes we start businesses with them. At other times we write books about them, just because the encounter has touched us so much that it fills us with joy, and that joy needs to flow out of us. At other times, they inspire us to create beautiful music or poetry or another form of art, and then they are called a muse. Soulmates bring us back to our truth, sometimes with a sentence or a word, or sometimes simply by being there and looking into our eyes. Soulmates are there to remind us there is a world of extreme beauty and inner peace that we all come from, a world that lives in each of us and to which we will all return to eventually. We see this other world when we look into the eyes of a soulmate, whoever they are, wherever they come from and however they show up in our lives.

When you meet a soulmate, it doesn't matter how long they stay with you. Receive the gift that meeting has for you and then simply look into their eyes, the very same eyes that hold the flame that made you recognise them, and say "Thank you", even if only in your mind. Be sure that a part of them has recognised you too and that part will receive the acknowledgement.

And once you have done this, let them go if they need to go. Respect that amazing connection for what it is. Don't try to make a romantic attachment out of it, if it's not meant to go that way. Don't try to force that person into your life or mould yours around them. Don't accept a job just because you felt this instant connection with the interviewer. Don't try to corrupt the beautiful energy of these encounters into a means to an end on your never-ending to-do lists, life plans and goals. Let it go where it wants to go and if it's just passing through your life, just say "Thank you" and receive the gift it brings you.

Because whenever they show up, and for however long they stay, they are there to help you walk your path.

I had always admired him. He was different than the rest of the managers there. Older, wiser, close to retirement, he was not afraid to speak his mind. He had a long list of achievements behind him; his value to the company was beyond question. And yet there was something else in him that shone in the authentic way in which he spoke in meetings, in the abrupt way he would sometimes deal with irritating colleagues. There was truth in him; he had discovered it inside himself and he was living it, unafraid.

People liked him and confided in him often. His office with its glass walls was always busy, with someone always seated in the empty chair he kept by his desk. People came to talk to him, ask for advice or simply offload their problems. He would listen and usually not talk too much. But the simple fact that he listened seemed to do the trick. People walked away feeling better.

I used to be one of them. I would take walks around the office and try to spot if his door was open, if he was on the phone or otherwise looked busy, if there was someone else in his office. When I spotted a good opportunity, I would stick my head in and say hi. He would stop whatever he was doing, sense there was something else in the air and tell me to come in and sit down for a while.

We would talk briefly, and it was usually about something completely different to what had led me to walk in there. I was stressed because I was not getting on with my boss. I could have asked him to talk to my boss about a certain situation, to help me out. But I did not. What he had for me was far more valuable than that. He gave me energy.

He did that effortlessly; it simply flowed out of him. He did that by simply being there, talking, listening. He did that as he prodded the conversation towards the topics that would interest me. We would talk about sailing, for instance, for just about ten minutes and then I would go out of his office feeling energised and ready to deal with whatever the day had in store for me.

And then, one day, he went away. I was on a conference call, one of those long, boring events with fifty people on the call. One of those things you can't escape from, but I had no real place in it either. I was there, at my desk, with the headphones on, looking absent-mindedly at the computer screen in front of me as I tried to make sense of the discussion happening in the background. The only input I had had in that call was to say hi when it started, and it was likely my next intervention would be to say bye just before I hung up.

I was stuck there on that call and I felt sad. Sad to be there, witnessing that call where stressed people fought for external power, sad to still be having problems with my boss no matter how much I tried to improve the situation, sad when I thought about the negative feedback I had recently received. I was sad that my time with that company was clearly approaching an end and I was sad when I thought of all the struggles it had been filled with. I felt discouraged and a bit lost, once again wondering what was it that I was doing with my life and why it felt so difficult sometimes.

And then I saw him. He walked past my desk and silently put a small, gift-wrapped box in front to me. I still had my headphones on and could not say a word, otherwise the whole conference call would have heard me.

"Merry Christmas," he said. "It comes early this year."

I was still speechless when he left. Christmas was not until the following week, it was still too early for presents, and I did not expect one from him anyway.

I opened it, while still on that call, with my headphones on. It was a sailing book; it was about the discovery of longitude. It had a small, handwritten note on the front page. It said it was meant to help me find my true north.

I felt tears in my eyes but I could not cry either, otherwise my sobs would have been heard on the conference call. I remembered what he told me once: "The joy is in the giving," he had said.

And true to that principle, he was not there when I had finished my call and I went to look for him to say thank you. He was not there the next day either, and someone told me it had been his last day in the company. He had decided to leave on early retirement.

But he was always there, in my life, from that moment onwards. We met again a few months later and had a coffee. Neither of us was working for that company any longer. Then, in a few more months, we met again. Our coffees turned into regular events, a few times a year. He became my mentor. I talked to him about business issues and about life choices. He listened, just as he always had when I used to visit his old office with glass walls. Sometimes he offered advice. Many times, he did not; he just smiled and let me talk.

When I told him I wanted to find a business opportunity in Argentina in a town called Lobos (which means 'wolves' in Spanish), he sent me another gift: the soundtrack of the movie Dances With Wolves. "To help you while packing your bags for the upcoming trip," he said. He was still there when I came back after that trip disillusioned, with my business plans in ashes. But having a coffee with him seemed to tell me, somehow, that it was not so tragic.

He was there for me many years afterwards, witnessing my falls and my recoveries, my path in life and my choices. He was there, just where he was meant to be, having a coffee with me a few times a year: no more. And the support that shone through in his presence has never ceased to amaze me.

The illusion of the wrong choice

We agonise so much over making decisions. We do this because of the paralysing fear of making the wrong one. How much more peace would we gain in our lives if we knew for sure there was no such thing as a wrong decision?

If we think of life as being a path we walk in order to learn, everything that happens to us, everything that we do or don't do, supports that learning. If a part of us feels we can benefit from an experience, we will choose it. The more conscious we are, the more conscious this choice will be and the easier it will be for us to accept the consequences. But even if we choose unconsciously, a part of us is always there to make the choice and it will do so for our greatest good.

Because everything that happens to us is there to serve us.

The bad things as well? Yep. The people who hurt us? Especially them. The wrong choices we make? Definitely. The problems we run into? Yes, them too.

Everything in our life is there because it serves us. One way or another, it helps us grow.

As we learn these lessons, we change the reality around us and a different set of situations and lessons present themselves to us. Sometimes the same situation will recur even when we have learned the lesson. Why is this happening? We are being tested. It's like a final exam. The universe says, "Ok, you have learned that lesson, but let's just see if you remember it well." And then we get a test. It's ok. It does not mean we are back to square one. It simply means we are being asked for a confirmation that we have learned a lesson.

When we look at life through these lenses, we stop seeing things as right or wrong, good or bad. We stop stressing about making the wrong decisions. All we need to do is live consciously; look after our own energy and honour what arises in us. The rest will take care of itself.

Turn to the end of the chapter and do exercise 7.1.

Consciousness

In the end, it's all about living consciously. About making conscious choices, about knowing where we are on our path and committing to never-ending learning.

You always know when you are not taking responsibility. But don't force yourself to do so if it does not come naturally. Don't beat yourself up. When you are not being authentic, simply notice this. When you lack integrity, be aware of it. And when you don't live your truth, know it. Accept yourself and where you are at this very moment.

That will be enough. Bringing consciousness to our day-to-day actions will raise our vibration. And when it rises, it will take us with it, our actions will change, the environments we live and work in will improve and the people around us will change too. And all this just because we raise our consciousness.

At work we are confronted with many situations when it's a matter of professional survival to not be authentic, to not be honest, to not take open responsibility. Don't beat yourself up for it. Don't carry the guilt around for ages after you let a meeting go in a certain direction because you have not had the courage to speak your mind. Or when you have not confronted the bad decision made just because you were afraid to lose your job. Remember we are all humans, and remember we are allowed to fail. There are times when we are allowed to be less than we can be. We are allowed to lose the path that points true north and then get back on it.

Whatever you have to do, do it consciously. The moments you fail, fail consciously. The moments you lack courage to be yourself, tell yourself: "I am lacking courage to be myself right now." And accept it. Without guilt, without self-punishment, just accept it. Love yourself as you do this. And know this will be enough.

Simply do your best. Day after day, hour after hour. Be aware of your energy and look after it. Pay attention to what arises in you and in your life and honour it. Walk your path, find your way, ask for help when you need it. Receive what life gives you and say thank you. Make your decisions, live your story, leave your legacy.

And as you do this, remember there is another definition of the word 'reflect': to throw something back, usually heat, light or sound, without absorbing it.

We are here to reflect the light that comes to us and grows in us, to send it all around us, to project it further and further, to let it shine though the darkest shadows on the earth. As it does so, the shadows shrink because darkness cannot stand light. And as you do this, you will feel you have achieved your purpose here. And the light you leave behind will keep on shining long after you are gone.

Summary: How to reflect

- Be aware of and continuously check where you are on your four main indicators:
    - Responsibility
    - Authenticity
    - Integrity
    - Honesty
- Look for feedback from life rather than from other people.
- When you feel like helping others, help yourself first.
- Remember that you are never alone.
- Recognise and honour soulmate connections and receive their gifts.
- Whatever choice you make, know it will be the right one.
- Live consciously and radiate the light around you.

Reflection Exercises:

7.1 Practise checking your course and adjusting your settings continuously:

- Sit down, ground, cleanse, protect and open your chakras.
- Ask yourself these questions:
  - ⇨ Am I taking responsibility for what is showing up in my life? How can I improve this?
  - ⇨ Am I being authentic in my life? How can I improve this?
  - ⇨ Am I acting from a place of integrity? Am I in touch with the whole of myself? How can I improve this?
  - ⇨ Am I being honest? With myself? With others? How can I improve this?
- Ask the questions one by one. After each question, pause and wait in silence. Focus on your breathing. Turn your attention to your heart as you wait for the answers to come. It is there where they will show up.
- Listen to what comes back. Ask further questions if needed.
- Say "Thank you".
- Check your grounding, close your chakras, open your eyes and carry on with your day.
- Do this every time you want to check if you're on the right track.

PART III
A Practical Guide to Using Energy in Corporate Situations

1. When you hold a meeting

Take a few moments to prepare yourself and the space for your meetings:

Before the meeting:
- Ground, cleanse and protect your own energy.
- Ground, cleanse and protect the room before the participants come in.
- In the case of conference calls, imagine the meeting room as a virtual meeting space where participants will interact with each other. Ground, cleanse and protect that space just as you would do with a physical space. Doing this will open an energetic space for that meeting to take place.
- Set your intention for this meeting. Use general outcomes rather than specific ones and add at the end of the intention a disclaimer: "If this is for the greatest benefit of all parties." Your intention can be that participants have an honest and open communication, that the best outcome for everyone present is achieved, and so on. Don't hold the intention to screw the other party over and ask for help on how to do this best. If you do, you will send out powerful negative energies into the world that will come back to you sooner or later.
- Take a moment to connect energetically to the participants before the meeting starts. Do this by visualising a white connection forming from your heart to the heart of each

participant. Keep the intention that this is done for the purpose and the duration of this meeting only and for the best interest of all parties.

- Respect other people's energy and free will. Never send a connection to someone with the intention to manipulate them into saying or doing anything.

During the meeting

- Ground often during the meeting. Ground before you start to speak and ground after you've just made a point. Whenever you don't know what to do or feel a bit lost, simply focus your attention inside your body and send it deep into the centre of the earth. A simple shortcut to help you ground is to be aware of the soles of your feet touching the floor.

After the meeting

- Take a moment to disconnect from the participants. See the white line that connects you dissolving and picture them going away.

- In your mind, say "Thank you" as you do this, irrespective of how thankful you are or are not to them in real life.

- Close the energy space you opened at the beginning of the meeting, say in your mind that it is now closed and send it upwards into the light.

- If you feel the need, take a moment to ground and cleanse again.

2. When you write a report or presentation

Writing can be one of the most stressful parts of our corporate jobs. Often we have to put our thoughts down on paper for reports, presentations, articles or summaries. Although we know the subject we are writing about, we usually spend a lot of time thinking about how to write, how to put these ideas down on paper, which structure to use, what slides to design. It does not need to be that difficult.

Take a moment to settle yourself into a creative state before you start writing:

- Ground, cleanse and protect your energy.

- Open your chakras.

- Set your intention about the report, presentation, article, or whatever you need to write. For instance: "I want to build a twenty-slide deck that best describes this project. I want the deck to be informative, easy to follow and to include the right level of detail for this audience."

- Spend some time visualising the report, the deck, the article or whatever you are creating. Don't visualise the content but give it a general form. See the pages, see the slides, see the chapters. See them as a light-shape, or as anything else that may come to mind.

- Cleanse them. Apply the same cleansing techniques you apply to your own energy or spaces. In your mind, bathe them with white light, wash them with water, get them under the shower, take a cloth and polish them. Do this until they are shining, sparkling clean.

- Then energise them. Visualise them in your hands or in front of you and ask for the white light to enter them, to fill them. Feel their weight increase in your hands as the energy enters them.

- Ground them. Visualise their roots, emerging from the shape you gave them and going down into the ground. If you need to, take their roots down and bind them separately to your own. Their roots and your roots are two different roots. They are created by you but they are not you. Bind their roots securely in the centre of the earth.

- Spend a moment feeling their weight, sensing how deeply anchored they are to the centre of the earth and admiring their shine.

- Then let them go; send them out in the universe.

- Open your eyes and start writing immediately, without thinking too much about it. Simply write the first sentences, design the first slide, or if it comes to you, write down the bullet-points of an outline. Start with what comes to your mind first and go from there, taking one step after another.

- Do that as fast as you can and without interruptions.

- As you write your words or design your slides, hold a feeling of detachment from them. Sit back a little. Let them come to you rather than chasing them. Trust that they will come. Don't try too hard, just express whatever comes through you.

- Go with this flow for as long as you are comfortable.

- When you feel it slowing down or stopping, close the writing session and start again another time.

- Take a moment to re-ground and close your chakras.

3. When you start or end something: initiatives, projects, jobs

Take a moment to start or end something energy-wise, in addition to what you do in your day-to-day life.

At the start

- Ground, cleanse and protect your energy.

- In your mind, form a positive intention for that initiative, project or job.

- Then let it go and don't think about it anymore.

- Start something new by letting yourself assimilate what comes to you. In a new job, let the knowledge build itself rather that following a script to gather it. When you talk to people to obtain information, let them tell you what they feel is important for you to know.

- Be open to this flow of information, without worrying too much about structuring it. Let it flow towards you and through you.

- Be alert to what grabs your attention, what touches you. When something does, stop the flow and look at that thing more closely. Ask questions, get more data, be curious about understanding it better. Trust that something has stirred your interest for a reason. Follow it and see where it leads you.

- Maintain this open and unstructured attitude for a few days at the start of a new job. Read the new energy that is coming towards you. Accept it. See where it wants to go and follow it.

- You can then gradually start to structure the information you have received, but be careful not to kill the incoming flow as you do so. Keep the flow open.

- Before you meet for the first time the people you are going to be working with or interacting with for that particular project, make sure you are in your power base and well-grounded, cleansed and protected.

- Establish an energetic connection with them (heart-to-heart, white line) before you meet them or speak to them for the first time.

- In your mind, form and hold the intention to make a good connection with them for the greatest good of all parties.

At the end

- Take time to properly say goodbye. Acknowledge what was good in others and in the project, what touched you, what you learned, what you appreciated. Don't worry about the negative parts. Just focus on the positive parts. When you finish something, it is important to leave it on a high energy note.

- After you do this in the real world, take some time to do it in your energy as well, in your mind, during your meditations. If there are things that have remained unsaid or if it was improper to do so in the real world, say them now. If you feel you need to say something to someone, imagine that person in front of you. Say thank you. Tell them what you appreciate about them. Tell them anything else you may feel it's important to say. If emotions come up, let them come. Cry if you have to. Hug them in your mind if you feel like it.

- When it comes to the people you conflicted with, imagine laughing with them about the troubles that you had, looking back and seeing it from a different perspective. You might have been adversaries but at the end of the game, you're going to share a beer and a chat. Don't worry if you feel you cannot perform this step. Simply acknowledge the lesson you learned, say thank you and let them go.

- Express everything that comes up to everyone in turn. Then see them going, one by one, and say thank you.

- When you are done saying farewell to the people, close off the energy space that the respective project, initiative or job has held in your life. Pack it up and send it to the light. See it going and see yourself letting it go.

- Allow yourself to feel sadness for a time. Don't suppress this. It's part of a healthy ending.

- Ground, cleanse and protect your energy again at the end of your farewell meditation. Come back into the here and now. And then live whatever this here and now has in store for you.

4. When you negotiate a deal

- From the very moment you are aware of a negotiation situation, work on finding, defining and strengthening your BATNA (Best Alternative To a Negotiated Agreement).

- Most of the time and effort you have available to prepare for the negotiation should be dedicated to strengthening your BATNA.

- On the day of the negotiation, make sure you ground, cleanse and protect thoroughly. Make sure your chakras are closed and have extra protection: anything like double doors in front of your chakras, placing shields in front of a door or imagining locking a door a few times can work.

- In your mind, form an intention that the best outcome for all parties may be reached.

- Feel this intention and then let it go.

- Enter the discussion, and remember to check your grounding frequently and readjust it if you feel the need. Stay inside your power base for the duration of the negotiation. That means keeping your awareness inside your body, feeling your body, feeling your soles on the floor. Feeling your weight. Feeling your feelings.

- Pay attention to all of your indicators as the discussion progresses and new alternatives are put on the table. Feel the response from your body, your emotions and your instincts regarding these proposals. Take a moment to go back inside and check how you feel.

- Ask yourself: what does my mind tell me? What does my body tell me? What does my gut tell me? What does my heart tell me?

- Also practise looking at 'the deal' as if it were one of the parties negotiating. Ask yourself, where does the deal want to go?

- Do not agree to proposals on the spot unless you are absolutely sure all your truth signals are on. Take the time that you need.

- At the end of the discussion, find a moment when you can be alone and ground, cleanse and protect again. Negotiations are usually intense situations where people actively try to influence each other to achieve outcomes that support their own ends, so your energy is likely to have been tampered with. Cleanse off anything that is not yours and recheck your protection.

5. When you make a decision

Practise making decisions from a place of wholeness, listening to the voices of all of your parts:

- Ground, cleanse, protect and open your chakras.
- Bring to mind a certain situation that requires a decision.
- Ask yourself these questions:
    - ⇨ What does my mind tell me?
    - ⇨ What does my gut tell me?
    - ⇨ What does my body tell me?
    - ⇨ What does my heart tell me?
- Listen to all the answers and note any differences.
- Then ask yourself if there is any other part in you that wants to speak and ask it to identity itself: who are you? Listen to what it has to say.
- If you feel the need to and believe in this, ask to speak to your spiritual guides. Visualise them around you and ask their opinions.
- Hold this council with the parts of yourself and your external guides for as long as you need to.
- If you feel you are still not sure about the decision, leave it there and commit yourself to coming back and checking on it later.
- Take time to do something else. This can be hours, days or weeks, depending on the type of decision you are facing.

- See if there is any *knowledge* that rises within you as you do this. Don't force it, simply notice it.

- Go back to talk to the parts of yourself and your guides at regular intervals, and alternate this with periods of not thinking about it entirely.

- As you do this, sooner or later the right decision will rise in you.

- When it does, check it, stay with it for a while, see how it feels. Make sure it is effortless and it fits naturally.

- Check if it increases or decreases your joy. This is the ultimate test. Make sure you don't confuse joy with enthusiasm. To check for joy, you need to take several joy measures and leave some time in between. Joy tends to be constant while enthusiasm comes and goes.

- Stay with it and keep checking on it until it becomes solid. Don't try to force it to solidify: just watch it and see where it wants to go.

- Once you are clear it is solid and well anchored in you, bring it out into the world as your decision.

6. When you deal with difficult people

- Ground, cleanse and protect your energy. Spend some extra time protecting it.

- In your mind, hold an intention to have your energy protected. Believe that what you are doing is enough and it will be protected.

- In your mind, visualise yourself surrounded by a bubble of white light and the other person surrounded by his own bubble. See the clear demarcation between your bubble and his bubble. Put a wall or a barrier in between and imagine it in any way it comes to you.

- When you meet with him, check your grounding often. Remember to stay inside your body and visualise your bubble of protection around you.

- If you sense something negative coming from him, visualise it ricocheting from the protective shield you have placed around your energy. Make sure you hold the intention that anything you reflect back is changed into positive energy. It does not matter how negative the energy he sends you is. It is in your best interests, as well as in those of everyone else, to only send out positive energy into the world.

- In case you detect the start of an emotional response – irritation or fear – it means he is starting to impact upon your energy. Reduce the time you spend with him or excuse yourself, leave the meeting and take a moment to breathe, adjust your grounding, check your cleansing and top up your protection. Wash off whatever touched your energy under a shower of white light.

- Go back inside your bubble, then go back to the room and continue the conversation if you have to.

- Remember to let go of the fear. It is your own fear that makes you vulnerable. Remember that whatever he sends you, it is only what you receive that touches you. Simply decide not to receive what you don't want.

- Resist any form of manipulation by remaining aware. Know when you are being threatened or when he is trying to intimidate you. Tell yourself in your mind, "He is trying to intimidate me now." Know it for what it is and this in itself will help you feel less affected by it.

- Don't try to teach him anything, make him better, make him see his mistakes or what he is doing to you. Doing so means you have to leave your protective bubble to go out to him, and you put yourself in a vulnerable position. There is no need for that. Everyone is responsible for his or her own energy and actions.

- Reduce the time you spend with difficult people to an absolute minimum. Remember, this is not about proving anything to yourself or the world. It takes energy to interact with difficult people and if you don't absolutely have to do it, don't. Keep your energy for something better.

7. When you work remotely

In today's corporations, working remotely has become an increasingly acceptable practice. It blends in better with people's lives; it makes them happier and more productive. Many corporations see the advantages, but on the other hand, many fear it will scatter the energy around and lose the feeling of cooperation, camaraderie and togetherness. Here's what you can do to make sure you stay connected:

- Ground, cleanse and protect your energy.

- Make sure you are in your body, with your energy home, every time you initiate a connection from a remote working place: when you send an email, work jointly with a colleague on a spreadsheet using modern collaboration techniques or call someone.

- Set up an energy connection to them (white line, heart-to-heart).

- Create a virtual space in your mind and call it 'office'. When you work from home, or from wherever you are, step into this mental space and tell yourself "I am now in the office, I am now connected to my colleagues for the purpose of this work."

- When you step out of it, tell yourself you have stepped out of it and that your energy returns to your home, holiday, or wherever you are and whatever you are doing.

- This can be done as many times throughout the day as required. It is important to keep in mind the intention to be 'in the work space' when you work, and the intention to leave it when you finish the work and go back to your house. That way you will function in two energy spaces and one will not influence the other.

- Allow for the flows of work and life to mix and mingle. If you have to follow certain timetables for meetings and calls, do so, but otherwise allow the 'work' time to rise in you naturally and don't constrain it to the socially acceptable nine-to-five concept, or to anything else you feel you should do because 'this is how it's done'.

- Hold the intention in your mind to do your work in the best possible way and then follow the sequence of steps that come to you. Take a break when you need it. Go back to your virtual workspace when you are drawn to it and go out of it when you feel you are done.

- Let yourself feel this flow and live with it. Do this with integrity.

Epilogue

This book came to me quickly, unexpectedly and powerfully. It rose effortlessly from all the knowledge I had accumulated, from all those work situations I had witnessed in the previous twenty years, and from all the experiments I had done with energy, both at work and in my personal life.

I did not call this book to me. I did not think I would write it, I did not prepare for it. I simply made space for it, and it came. And the circumstances of my personal life had arranged themselves so that it had the time and the space it needed to come out.

I trusted the process and let it out of me. I send it out now into the world. I let it go where it wants to go. I am not trying to teach anything to anyone. I am not trying to help. I am not saying that this approach is right for all. I only say it has worked for me, and while doing this I have often found it reinforced by what others spoke or wrote about. To me, it makes sense. For me, it works.

I have seen other people apply these principles and do so in their unique way. I know of others who ground, cleanse and protect their energy and do this using their own scenarios or visualisation techniques. I know of people who spend a few minutes a day doing this and of others who are lost in meditations for hours.

It doesn't matter how you do it or what framework you use. Whether my seven steps, as presented in this book, make sense to you or whether you feel you should add another one or two. It doesn't matter if you do the exercises in this book in the order presented or not, or if you use the visualisations I recommend. It doesn't even matter if you don't do them at all; if you choose to walk a different path.

What really matters is your awareness. Know your energy. Trust it. Make time to rediscover it and make a commitment to be true to it. Look after it, own it, love it.

In the end, all that matters is how we bring love into this world, and the first and most important step is self-love.

Dictionary of key concepts

Aura – electromagnetic field that surrounds the body of every person, every organism and object in the universe. For a person it will be around the size of their outstretched arms. Some trained psychics can see the auras of other people. Kirlian photography can actually capture it.

Chakra – comes from Sanskrit and means 'wheel'. There are seven chakras, or energy centres, in our bodies and it is through these gateways that our energy spins and flows in and out. Awareness of these energy centres and their attributes can assist greatly with personal energy management.

Energy – life force or energy, is the essence of our being, our consciousness, our soul. Different traditions or disciplines have different names for it, but they all refer to the same concept:
- Chinese = Chi or Qi
- Japanese = Ki
- Sanskrit = Prana
- Greek = Pneuma
- Hawaiian = Mana
- Technical = Bio-energy, subtle energy, primary energy
- Western = Ether, animal magnetism, vital force
- Other names for it = Psychic energy, magical energy, universal energy

    Energy is also expressed as attention, awareness or focus. Where your thoughts go, energy will follow.

Energy cords – Throughout our lives, both positive and negative energy cords are established between us and people, animals, places, situations/experiences and thought forms. The negative cords deplete our energy, weaken our aura and can block our chakras, causing physical and emotional issues.

Intuition – The sum of all the messages you receive, either consciously or unconsciously. Includes rationality and instinct but extends to incorporate energy, spiritual and emotional messages as well.

Intention – the energy that we send in a certain direction via thought and/or wish. Includes, but is not limited to, plans, desires, fears, outcomes, purposes.

Manifestation – the ability to attract effortlessly the things we desire in our lives.

Acknowledgements

My thanks and gratitude to the School of Intuition and Healing in London for the wonderful courses that have built my understanding of the world of energy and encouraged me to apply these principles in the corporate world.

I would also like to thank Emily, Agnes, Kristin, Brendan and Michael for the very helpful suggestions and feedback on the early versions of this book.

From the same author

Through Dust and Dreams, 2014

At a crossroads in her life, Roxana decides to take a ten-day safari trip to Africa. In Namibia, she meets a local guide who talks about "the courage to become who you are" and tells her that "the world belongs to those who dream".

Her holiday over, Roxana still carries the spell of his words within her soul. Six months later she quits her job and searches for a way to fulfil an old dream: crossing Africa from north to south. Teaming up with Richard and Peter, two total strangers she meets over the internet, Roxana starts a journey that will take her and her companions from Morocco to Namibia, crossing deserts and war-torn countries and surviving threats from corrupt officials and tensions within their own group.

Through Dust and Dreams is the story of their journey: a story of courage and friendship, of daring to ask questions and search for answers, and of self-discovery on a long, dusty road south.

www.throughdustanddreams.com

About the author

Roxana Valea is a management consultant, Reiki and energy medicine practitioner, entrepreneur and author. She is based in London and Mallorca but travels the world frequently and works remotely from other locations. Over the past 20 years she has built her business career as a corporate employee, entrepreneur and freelance consultant. Her management consultancy company, Value Associates, specialises in business transformation. She has an MBA degree from SDA Bocconi, one of the top business schools in Europe and has delivered consulting projects for well-known companies (Apple, Sony, eBay amongst others) as well as top consulting companies (Roland Berger Strategy Consultants and Proudfoot Consulting). In her work as a management consultant she believes in a blend of traditional consulting methodologies with the intuitive aspects of energy manifestation. As an author she has written travel journals, novels and business books.

www.roxanavalea.com